50

WAYS TO USE
TECHNOLOGY
ENHANCED
LEARNING
IN THE CLASSROOM

50

WAYS TO USE TECHNOLOGY ENHANCED LEARNING IN THE CLASSROOM

PRACTICAL STRATEGIES FOR TEACHING

PETE ATHERTON

Learning Matters
An imprint of SAGE Publications Ltd
1 Oliver's Yard
55 City Road
London EC1Y 1SP

SAGE Publications Inc.
2455 Teller Road
Thousand Oaks, California 91320

SAGE Publications India Pvt Ltd
B 1/I 1 Mohan Cooperative Industrial Area
Mathura Road
New Delhi 110 044

SAGE Publications Asia-Pacific Pte Ltd
3 Church Street
#10-04 Samsung Hub
Singapore 049483

Editor: Amy Thornton
Production controller: Chris Marke
Project management: Swales & Willis Ltd, Exeter, Devon
Marketing manager: Lorna Patkai
Cover design: Wendy Scott
Typeset by: C&M Digitals (P) Ltd, Chennai, India
Printed in the UK

First published 2018

Library of Congress Control Number: 2017954852

British Library Cataloguing in Publication Data

A catalogue record for this book is available from the British Library

ISBN 978-1-5264-2414-3
ISBN 978-1-5264-2415-0 (pbk)

At SAGE we take sustainability seriously. Most of our products are printed in the UK using FSC papers and boards. When we print overseas we ensure sustainable papers are used as measured by the PREPS grading system. We undertake an annual audit to monitor our sustainability.

Contents

About the author

Pete Atherton has been an educator for over twenty years. An English teacher by trade, he has also taught media and film studies. He is now a lecturer and tutor on the PGCE at Liverpool John Moores and Edge Hill University. His Master's dissertation examined technology enhanced learning and formative assessment. His PHD thesis is about how social media tools and data can help disseminate academic research.

Pete lives in Liverpool with his wife, Linda and his two children, Max and Joe.

@Petestarryid on Twitter

Email: Peteath@hotmail.com

Acknowledgements

I would like to thank the many people who have given me inspiration or made encouraging sounds when I have told them my ideas. In no particular order: Emy Onuora for showing me the way, Dr Vicky Duckworth from Edge Hill University for starting this happy ball rolling, Jo Watson from A Goodwriteup, and Mike Graham and Rob Clarke for helping me feel that I could make this a success. I also salute Amy Thornton from Learning Matters for endless patience and effortless cool and Caroline Watson from Swales & Willis for forensic attention to detail. I'd also like to thank my trainee teachers at Liverpool John Moores University for their inspiration and courage.

Most of all, I'd like to thank Linda – my beautiful rock, Max and Joe – my peerless sons, and all my family who have allowed everything else to function with great joy.

Introduction

You are unlikely to use all 50 of these ideas in your teaching. You should, however, find something in each chapter that can help you teach better, assess more efficiently or enjoy using educational technology (edtech).

As an experienced teacher, it started to occur to me in the mid-noughties that learners were developing skills that were neither recognised nor celebrated by their teachers at any level – me included. Initially I would rail against the practice of students googling simple answers, without checking the results, instead of sticking to tried and tested methods. I eventually realised that I was fighting a losing battle: these old methods had been tried and tested but seemed to have little or no place in the modern world.

This realisation led many teachers to a crisis of confidence: if the teacher's role is no longer the keeper of the gates of knowledge, then what are teachers for? By the start of the 2010s I realised that a quiet revolution had taken place. The unspoken rules of teaching and learning had been rejected and dismantled by learners but apparently reinforced by policymakers, with whom teachers were under ever more pressure to comply. In the middle were edtech providers, who were improvising, innovating, building brand equity and engaging in dialogue with educators, institutions and sometimes politicians.

This book has been written to support you to use edtech in a way that actually helps your learners. It is also designed to provide you with the skills and mindset to embrace rapid changes in the culture of learning. In this introduction we will firstly summarise the structure of each chapter, then allow a glimpse into some of the themes explored in the book. After reading the book, you should have a clearer sense of how to ensure that your use of edtech is always linked to meaningful formative assessment. You should also feel empowered to know how to use a selection of edtech tools, and why. It is not a complete guide, nor could it ever be. Indeed, some aspects of edtech are omitted altogether (for example, Massive Open Online Courses, or MOOCs). The vast number of available resources is changing the way we teach, but is it changing the way we learn?

The chapters are organised into the following overlapping categories:

- recent and emerging themes in edtech;
- assessment/assignment tools;
- social media;
- video and audio;

- collaborative working;

- games and learner response systems;

- presentation.

Each chapter that tackles a specific edtech platform will be structured in the following way:

- what is (the name of the edtech tool)?;

- an infographic summarising the benefits of using it;

- what can it do for teachers and learners?;

- how to use it;

- how to assess using it;

- how it fits into the broader socio-cultural context (a short literature review);

- how you can use it to meet the secondary Teachers' Standards (Gov.uk, 2012).

Broader themes

One of the themes that presents itself through the literature is the notion that knowledge about digital technologies changes when we are close to understanding it. Digital technologies are always fluid; when a new technology emerges it is already likely to be rendered obsolete by some other innovation. Moreover, each emerging technology is likely to develop in its functionality and sophistication.

The myth of Proteus is sometimes invoked as a framing device for the problems teachers face when trying to keep up with new technologies. In Greek mythology, Proteus was a sea god, who had the gift of omniscience. Proteus changed shape, taking an elusive liquid form, which made him virtually impossible to catch (Raffaghelli et al., 2015).

If the aim of this book were to capture technology like Proteus and explain it to the reader, it would fail. Instead of attempting this, the book will instead evaluate how to improve teachers' use of technology enhanced learning (TEL). In a swiftly changing culture, we will analyse some of the ways in which teachers could create lessons and teaching episodes that may be collaborative and enjoyable but also help assess their learners and improve their thinking skills. In doing so, the book will make recommendations on how teachers can use TEL to help them plan their questions with formative assessment, mastery and high-order thinking in mind.

We will soon explore some of the tools available to teachers. Firstly, though, we will ensure that we all understand the meaning and context of some of the broader concepts that will be referred to throughout the book. The first will be how social media can be used as a learning tool. The book will also examine the rapid development of artificial intelligence in education, gamified learning, flipped learning and the growing use of comparative judgements to assess students' work. The remainder of the book will address individual apps and tools.

References

Gov.uk (2012). *Teachers' Standards*. Available online at: https://www.gov.uk/government/publications/teachers-standards [accessed 23 September 2017].

Raffaghelli, J, Cucchiara, S, Persico, D (2015) Methodological approaches in MOOC research: retracing the myth of Proteus. Special issue: Massive Open Online Courses (MOOCs): 'disrupting' teaching and learning practices in higher education May 2015. *British Journal of Educational Technologies*, 46(3): 488–509.

Edtech will always change – quickly

1

Formative assessment in the digital age

This chapter will assess how formative assessment is evolving in the digital age.

Formative assessment is also referred to as assessment for learning (or AFL). Black and Wiliam (2010) defined the term more rigorously; assessment for learning can only give way to formative assessment when the feedback provided determines the teacher's ensuing actions. Boyle and Charles (2013) identified

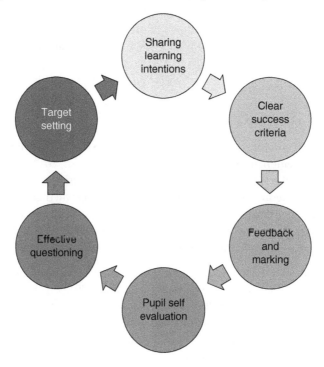

Image 1.1 Does edtech help or hinder the process of AFL?

wide variations in teachers' definitions of formative assessment. The literature was similarly varied: Coffey et al. (2011, cited in Boyle and Charles, 2013, p8) defined formative assessment as using a genuine engagement with ideas to determine a teacher's next steps. Popham (2008, cited in Boyle and Charles, 2013) sees formative assessment as different from summative assessment in that it is designed to produce a qualitative score, not a grade.

When each chapter examines an educational technology (edtech) platform or tool, we will discuss its potential to help teachers assess. One of the enduring debates will be to what extent edtech reinforces or challenges the old methods of AFL, summarised above.

Indeed, there is considerable debate about how best to use formative assessment among a generation of 'digital natives', who have been raised using digital technologies (Prensky, 2001). According to Blink (2015), edtech tools are more likely to be successful if teachers learn how to use the data to enable progression, which would require ongoing training (Higgins et al., 2011; Passey, 2014).

Indeed, Prensky (2010) argues that formative assessment is only worth the considerable effort if learners read it, think about it and act upon it (Prensky, 2010, p176). Though edtech is frequently associated with distance learning, effective formative assessment still requires dialogue and feedback (William, 2011; Boyle and Charles, 2013). Black and Wiliam (2010) argued that the constant drive to grade, rank and improve is currently at the expense of useful advice and the learning function (Black and Wiliam, 2010).

Furthermore, digital technologies can open up opportunities to go beyond formative assessment. For example, 'ipsative assessment' relates to the practice of stretching and challenging learners by encouraging them to beat their personal best (Prensky, 2010, p176). Though this method is borrowed from sport, it could be adapted by edtech platforms by focusing the challenge on certain skills. The instant data generated by many edtech assessment tools could facilitate this more helpful form of analysis.

Formative assessment and policy

As summative levels were abolished as the dominant form of assessment, schools and colleges are instructed to place greater emphasis on formative assessment (McIntosh, 2015). For teachers, formative assessment is described in the *Final Report of the Commission on Assessment Without Levels* as enabling teachers to plan and evaluate their teaching in terms of establishing whether their learning is stalling or thriving (McIntosh, 2015). Under the new National Curriculum, learners must experience formative assessment on small units of work before progressing to the next (Fleming, 2012; McIntosh, 2015). The emphasis, therefore, is on deeper understanding of learners' strengths and struggles.

The endgame, therefore, is to reach 'mastery learning', which prioritises a deeper, consolidated understanding of fewer topics (Guskey, 2012, cited in McIntosh, 2015). This is a development from the notion of 'deep learning' (Entwistle, 2000, cited in Scales, 2013) and may necessitate clear communication of a lesson's 'mastery goals' at the start (Hattie, 2008). Though Ofsted recognise the importance of formative assessment, they do not dictate how much or how frequently formative assessment should take place (McIntosh, 2015).

Edtech and mastery?

Could edtech serve as a catalyst to mastery learning? Saidi (2015) argues that the subsequent summative assessment could create learner anxiety, even a broader insecurity towards their educational existence. Black and Wiliam (2010) indicated that *the giving of marks and grading function are overemphasized, while the giving* of *useful advice and the learning function are underemphasized* (cited in Saidi, 2015, p6).

In terms of the latest Government drives towards reforming how formative assessment is managed, recorded and acted upon, there is a move away from the idea of 'fixed ability' and a focus on skills, knowledge and understanding (McIntosh, 2015, pp27–28). As teachers assess without levels, there may need to be a fine balance between the availability of data and its relevance. To what extent does extensive data help children learn?

Digital dependency?

There is a tension between the need for teachers to acquire and update new skills and the fear that learners are being effectively de-skilled through their digital dependency (Gardner and Davis, 2013). Though digital natives are demonstrating advanced skills in multitasking at speed, there is a fear that the skill of metacognition – or thinking about thinking – is being atrophied or eroded. The paucity of empirical evidence from the UK in this area may suggest that more is needed if these ideas are to inform Government policy (Helsper and Eynon, 2009). Indeed, the Commission for Assessment without Levels (McIntosh, 2015), the Carter Review (Carter, 2015) and the response to the Carter Review (Morgan, 2016; Munday, 2016) made no reference at all to the changing ways in which digital natives learn. Though Ofsted and Government policy continue to have a great deal to say about formative assessment, it may be time to look more closely at how edtech can accelerate and enrich the process.

References

Black, P and Wiliam, D (2010) Inside the black box: raising standards through classroom assessment. *Phi Delta Kappan*, 92(1): 81–90.

Blink, RJ (2015) *Leading Learning for Digital Natives: Combining Data and Technology in the Classroom.* London: Routledge.

Boyle, B, Charles, M (2013) *Formative Assessment for Teaching and Learning.* London: SAGE.

Carter, A (2015) *Carter Review of Initial Teacher Training (ITT).* Available online at: https://www.gov.uk/government/uploads/system/uploads/attachment_data/file/399957/Carter_Review.pdf [accessed 16 August 2017].

Fleming, P (2012) *Becoming a Secondary School Teacher: How to Make a Success of Your Initial Teacher Training and Induction,* 2nd edition. London: Routledge.

Gardner, H, Davis, K (2013) *The App Generation.* New Haven, CT: Yale University Press.

Hattie, J (2008) *Visible Learning: A Synthesis of Over 800 Meta-Analyses Relating to Achievement*. London: Routledge.

Helsper, E, Eynon, R (2009) Digital natives: where is the evidence? *British Educational Research Journal*, 1–18. DOI: 10.1080/01411920902989227.

Higgins, S, ZhiMin, X, Katsipataki, M (2011) *The Impact of Digital Technology on Learning: A Summary for the Education Endowment Foundation*. Available online at: https://v1.educationendowmentfoundation. org.uk/uploads/pdf/The_Impact_of_Digital_Technologies_on_Learning_FULL_REPORT_%282012%29. pdf [accessed 16 August 2017].

McIntosh, K (2015) *Final Report of the Commission on Assessment without Levels*. Available online at: https://www.gov.uk/government/uploads/system/uploads/attachment_data/file/483058/ Commission_on_Assessment_Without_Levels_-_report.pdf [accessed 15 August 2016].

Morgan, N (2016) *Strengthening the quality and content of initial teacher training (ITT): the development of a framework of content for ITT; behaviour management content; and standards for school-based ITT mentors*. Gov.uk. Available online at: https://www.gov.uk/government/uploads/system/uploads/attachment_ data/file/536916/Govt_response_-_ITT.pdf [accessed 17 August 2017].

Munday, S (2016) *A Framework of Core Content for Initial Teacher Training (ITT)*. Available online at: https://www.gov.uk/government/uploads/system/uploads/attachment_data/file/536890/Framework_ Report_11_July_2016_Final.pdf [accessed 16 August 2017].

Passey, D (2014) *Inclusive Technology Enhanced Learning*. London: Routledge.

Prensky, M (2001) Digital natives, digital immigrants, part I. *On the Horizon*, 9(5): 1–6.

Prensky, M (2010) *Teaching Digital Natives*. London: SAGE.

Saidi, A (2015) *Using Formative Assessment and Social Media for Effective Learning*. Available online at: https://gupea.ub.gu.se/bitstream/2077/38432/1/gupea_2077_38432_1.pdf [accessed 16 August 2017].

Scales, P (2013) *Teaching in the Lifelong Learning Sector*, 3rd edition. Maidenhead: Open University Press.

William, D (2011) *Embedded Formative Assessment 228*, 2nd edition. Bloomington, IN: Solution Tree.

2
Gamification

Why gamified learning?

The notion of learning through play is, of course, as old as learning itself. On a simple level, the appeal of learning through games is that participants' level of engagement is so high, they are unaware that they are learning (Wang, 2014). While it is axiomatic that young children learn through playing, it is also true that older children and even adults often desire and even expect their learning to be gamified.

Before examining the concept of gamification (or gamified learning) in depth, it is worth noting that several edtech platforms discussed in this book can be seen as educational games. Kahoot! and A Tale Unfolds are notable examples. It may also be helpful to point out that this book extols the virtues of combining online activities with offline, or visual with kinaesthetic. An example of this is how any sort of game can provide important features of experiential learning: the 'concrete experience' of an absorbing game and the 'active experimentation' of doing something to demonstrate the learning (Kolb, 1984).

Gamification, or gamified learning, incorporates the aesthetics and functionality of games (Kapp et al., 2012) to engage, educate and motivate learners (Kiryakova et al., 2014). All users are active participants – their progress is recorded and ranked. Increasingly, empirical data can track and reward with virtual badges or medals (Kiryakova et al., 2014). Teachers will be aware that games can provide a little 'fun' for the class. Is gamified activity, though, likely actually to help learners? Will they be more motivated and will they learn better this way? This debate is crucial to some discussions of teaching and learning.

Studies into gamified learning

Cognitive factors

Gamification could help improve the 'intrinsic motivation' of learners. Deci and Ryan referred to three aspects of intrinsic motivation (Deci and Ryan, 2008, cited in Dron and Anderson, 2015): if a learning task gives learners a sense of control, is within their range of competence and enables them to relate to others. This will create the correct climate for intrinsic motivation to occur. Gamified platforms usually enable learners to control their answer in a quiz or next action in a narrative. Games present levels of challenge, starting with easy, manageable tasks. Games are social in that they can be competitive or collaborative.

Emotional factors

Moreover, if learners begin to see failure as less of a negative and more of a formative opportunity (Kolb, 1984), this can further improve their engagement. Completion and success rates have been seen to be significantly higher when learners are placed in groups that offer networks of mutual support (Deci and Ryan, 2008, cited in Dron and Anderson, 2015).

Gamification works on a series of principles of how the channels in the brain process sounds and images. Though educators may be wary of applying cognitive science to learning, the next idea could help explain some of the pitfalls of gamification. The Split Attention Principle emphasises the need for spoken words to accompany images and video on a screen. The Redundancy Principle, however, states that too many stimuli can hinder learning. An example of this is the presence of animation alongside spoken language and text (Tettegah, 2015). Barriers to learning create anxiety and frustration, especially amongst learners who may use technology as an escape from social reality. Careful management of emotions is essential to the success of computer-aided learning.

The potential emotional benefits for learners are the challenge of the questions and thinking time, the reward of viewing participants' scores on the board and the competition of the visible ranking (Kocadere, 2015). Further potential emotional rewards are the harmony of teamwork, and the acquisition of, feedback from and validation by points and leaderboards (Kocadere, 2015). Gamification can improve learners' motivation (Deci and Ryan, 2008, cited in Dron and Anderson, 2015) and develop skills that go much deeper than learning by rote (Dale, 2014, cited in Featherstone, 2015).

Critics of gamified platforms, however, warn against how the creation of hierarchical league tables can be divisive within a group (Kocadere, 2015). In addition to this risk, there is a danger of the class experiencing diminishing returns from game-based edtech (Wang, 2014).

References

Dron, J, Anderson, T (2015) *Teaching Crowds: Learning and Social Media*. Edmonton, AB: AU Press.

Featherstone, M (2015) *Using Gamification to Enhance Self-Directed, Open Learning in Higher Education*. Available online at: http://shura.shu.ac.uk/12638/93/Featherstone%20Using%20 Gamification%20 to%20Enhance%20Learning.pdf [accessed 16 August 2017].

Kapp, K, Blair, L, Mesch, R (2013) *The Gamification of Learning and Instruction Fieldbook: Ideas into Practice*. San Francisco: Wiley.

Kiryakova, G, Angelova, N, Yordanova, L (2014) Gamification in education. *Proceedings of 9th International Balkan Education and Science Conference*.

Kocadere, S (2015) The design and implementation of a gamified assessment. *Journal of e-Learning and Knowledge Society*, 11(3): 1–2. Available online at: http://je-lks.org/ojs/index.php/Je-LKS_EN/article/view/1070 [accessed 16 August 2017].

Kolb, DA (1984) *Experiential Learning: Experience as the Source of Learning and Development*. Englewood Cliffs, NJ: Prentice Hall.

Tettegah, S (2015) *Emotions, Technology, and Learning (Emotions and Technology)*. Oxford: Elsevier.

Wang, A (2014) The wear out effect of a game-based student response system. *Computers & Education*, 82: 1–22. Available online at: http://www.sciencedirect.com/science/article/pii/S0360131514002516 [accessed 16 August 2017].

3
The flipped classroom

What is the 'flipped classroom'?

Also referred to as 'flipped learning', the 'flipped classroom' is an inevitable by-product of the preponderance of digital technologies in post-industrial societies. It is a method of teaching in which the traditional model is inverted. Traditionally, the teacher – a *sage on the stage* (Morrison, 2014) – disseminated knowledge in a classroom, then set homework to cement learners' understanding.

In the flipped classroom, work is completed under the guidance of the teacher in a classroom environment but only after learners have absorbed various online resources at home. Like many aspects of edtech, it should be handled with care, with careful planning, testing and evaluation. The consequences of jumping in with both feet could be embarrassing at best, damaging for the learners at worst.

A radical change?

The challenge of flipping the classroom was to create something both radical in its delivery and profound in its effects. According to Scheg (2015), the flipped classroom is part of a radical change, or *paradigm shift*, where electronic learning (e-learning) is naturally embedded into everyday education. The 'collective space' of a classroom becomes less of an arena for instruction, to be consumed passively. Instead, it becomes more dynamic, with the teacher facilitating activities, rather than delivering content. The content can then develop more creatively and interactively.

If teachers are freed up to spend more time helping students individually, they should foster better relationships with their learners and put them at ease. Learners can pause and rewind materials if they struggle and work at their own pace, which helps with differentiation. Learners can develop a greater sense of control (Kurtz, 2014); this method *transfers responsibility* (Kurtz, 2014) for online study from the classroom to anywhere with an internet router. At best, the flipped classroom could create an almost utopian dream of a collaborative, harmonious and higher-achieving cohort. It could also relieve some of the pressure on teachers to 'perform'. The emphasis, therefore, can be on a personalised education (Bergmann, 2012).

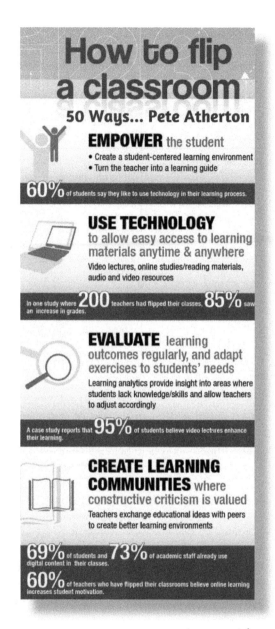

Image 3.1 Infographic: the flipped classroom

Infographic adapted from a US public domain blog: **http://tsaponar.blogspot.co.uk/2014/02/how-to-flip-classroom-infograp**

The effects of using digital technologies are advantageous and pernicious at the same time (Taylor, 2012). On one hand, frequent internet use limits learners' attention spans. If we are not paying attention, there is little chance of developing our cognitive skills. On the other hand, the infinite web of available information removes the need to *retain* information. Learners are freed up to develop 'high-order' thinking, for example, *contemplation, critical thinking, and problem solving* (Taylor, 2012). Attitudes towards young people's prolific use of digital technology, then, are persistently ambivalent.

Table 3.1 Traditional versus 'flipped' classroom

Traditional classroom: teacher-centred	Flipped classroom: learner-centred	Benefits of flipped classroom	Risks of flipped classroom
Students sit in rows	Students can work anywhere on mobile devices	Better sense of self-actualisation	Less control over production of work
Information is presented	Problem-based tasks	A more individual and differentiated approach to learning	They still have to study the materials
All students get the same information	Personalised responses are encouraged	Fosters high-order thinking	Potential for shyness
Learning outcomes are static, finite	Learning outcomes are interdisciplinary	Encourages thirst for knowledge	Weaker, less-motivated students will need careful handling
About facts	Synagogy - students collaborate in content creation	Ownership of knowledge	Students may feel less secure

Adapted from **www.centeril.org** (open source).

Learners taking control of their education through the flipped classroom is one way in which they can represent their own interests. However, the converse can also be true: if the flipped classroom prescribes a diet of targeted and finite resources to be digested beforehand, it could be argued that this action not only controls learners' behaviour – making them more solitary and domestic – but also leaves them more open to knowledge which is frequently bankrolled by corporate entities with ties to politicians. Indeed, as reported by *Politico* magazine in February 2015, corporations like Pearson are already wielding control over the US education system; in 2001, US Congress passed the No Child Left Behind Act, which gave Pearson unprecedented access to the distribution of educational resources (Simon, 2015). Further reforms, for example online learning, helped Pearson's US sales to soar to $4billion. In the UK Edexcel are owned by Pearson. In 2011 *The Telegraph* revealed that Edexcel generated a turnover of £317m (Watt and Newell, 2011). Could it be that the skills acquired through more independent learning empower young people to identify and potentially dismantle traditional power structures?

References

Bergmann, J (2012) *Flip Your Classroom: Reach Every Student in Every Class*. Savannah, GA: International Society for Technology in Education.

Kurtz, G (2014) The flipped-classroom approach: the answer to future learning? *European Journal of Open, Distance and Elearning*, 1: 1–10. Available online at: http://www.eurodl.org/?p=current&article=661 [accessed 20 August 2015].

Morrison, CD (2014) From 'sage on the stage' to 'guide on the side': a good start. *International Journal for the Scholarship of Teaching and Learning,* 8: 1.

Scheg, A (2015) *Implementation and Critical Assessment of the Flipped Classroom Experience.* Hershey, PA: Information Science Reference.

Simon, S (2015) No profit left behind. *Politico,* 1: 1–2. Available online at: http://www.politico.com/ story/2015/02/pearson-education-115026 [accessed 12 October 2015].

Taylor, J (2012 How technology is changing the way children think and focus. *Psychology Today,* 1: 1–5. Available online at: https://www.psychologytoday.com/blog/the-power-prime/201212/how-technology-is-changing-the-way-children-think-and-focus [accessed 1 September 2015].

Watt, H, Newell, C (2011) *Exam Boards: Edexcel Went from Charity to £1bn Business.* Available online at: http://www.telegraph.co.uk/education/secondaryeducation/8943761/Exam-boards-Edexcel-went-from-charity-to-1bn-business.html [accessed 11 August 2017].

4

Bring your own device (BYOD)

Why BYOD?

In the 1990s, educational establishments were in a position to make suites of PCs or Macs available for use. This prized resource would have to be pre-booked and was frequently double-booked, much to the frustration of teachers and students alike. The network was often slow and the internet was usually unreliable, sometimes woefully so. The noughties brought wifi and laptops but the problems of accessibility and connectivity persisted. As the take-up of smartphones and tablets gained momentum, so did the drive for both staff and learners to bring their own devices to class. The complex set of circumstances and issues related to this will be unpicked in this chapter.

Universal tech?

If learners are to be encouraged to bring their own devices, many teachers will be concerned that poorer children could miss out on exciting learning episodes. Schools can, at times, be absolute in their judgements about how much digital technology their learners can access. Teachers in deprived schools can overinflate their perception of scarcity, while the opposite can be the case in the better-resourced leafy suburbs.

Looking at some facts may help clarify your position on the feasibility of BYOD. Ofcom's (2016) report revealed that 98% of all 12–15-year-olds have access to the internet at home (Ofcom, 2016, p30), 80% of 8–11-year-olds and 74% of 11–15-year-olds were in possession of a tablet and 79% owned a smartphone (Ofcom, 2016, pp26–27). The same report provides a glimpse into the adoption of devices such as smartphones. In 2013, 61% of 12–15-year-olds owned a smartphone but 20% had a phone that was non-smartphone (that is, it was fast internet-enabled). This figure changed to 79% with a smartphone and only 6% without by 2016. It appears that the trend is heading towards universal take-up of smartphones.

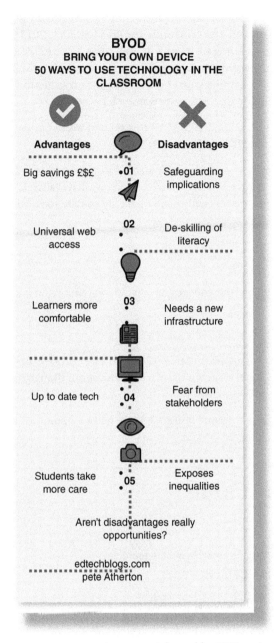

Image 4.1 Infographic: BYOD – advantages and disadvantages

Budget cuts

Another potential driver for adopting a BYOD policy is a perception of swingeing cuts to school and college budgets. Again, that may need to be deconstructed through some facts.

Though average spending per secondary pupil rose by 5% a year during the 2000s, it is expected to fall by 6.5% between 2015 and 2020 (Institute for Fiscal Studies, 2017). In further education, the picture is more dramatic: spending per learner is 10% lower than in secondary but in 1990, average further education spending was 45% higher. Also, spending in school sixth forms has fallen by 18% from 2011 (Institute for Fiscal Studies, 2017, p21). This runs counter to the Government's claims of fairness and protected funding on the Gov.uk website (Gov.uk, 2017).

Spending on edtech, however, appears to buck this downward trend, as it is expected to grow from £45bn in 2015 to £129bn in 2020 (Moules, 2015).

Despite an apparent increase in spending on edtech, some teachers may feel that a lot of the money has not had much of an impact and hardware has been wasted (Paddick, 2016). This is where BYOD could save the taxpayer, as learners will usually have up-to-date tech, which they will certainly feel comfortable using.

Policies on BYOD

As you may be aware, schools and colleges have wildly varying policies towards using smartphones in school.

What happens when you adopt a BYOD policy?

RM Education's 2016 survey revealed that 29% of secondary schools have a BYOD policy and 26% are considering adopting BYOD (Ofcom, 2016). RM Education, though, do have a vested interest in helping schools with their IT solutions.

However institutions address the issue of BYOD, there will be a potential minefield of factors to consider, as illustrated below.

The realities of BYOD

Fear

- What are the implications in terms of safeguarding?
- How might BYOD change these?

Policy

- How might BYOD change the policy on mobile phone use in lessons?
- How is the school going to ensure that they are not de-skilling children in terms of literacy and numeracy?

Parents and other stakeholders

- What might parents and stakeholders have to say? How will you engage with them and continue to address their concerns and create opportunities?

Infrastructure

- How will it work?
- How good is the wifi?
- Has the project been tested, piloted?

Who pays for the infrastructure?

- How much will it cost over a 5-10-year period?
- How are the funding, outgoings and revenue streams likely to change over that time?

What is also worth critiquing is OECD's (2015) claim that frequent computer use has a damaging effect on learners' progress. If this is the case, greater emphasis may need to be placed on learners acquiring the skills to navigate their way through online content. This is similar to the ideas about how the 'connectivist' classroom will necessitate the building of the ability to manage potentially infinite content and turn it into mastery of knowledge (Siemens, 2005; Downes, 2007; Donnelly, 2010).

Summary

However a school or college approaches BYOD, they may want to think carefully about the personnel who will create, measure, review and improve its impact. It would be incumbent on the staff and stakeholders to create a clear strategy. For this to happen, the right people will need the right incentives and support. Without the right infrastructure, how could BYOD possibly be a workable solution (Paddick, 2016)?

References

Donnelly, R, Harvey, J, O'Rouke, K (2010) *Critical Design and Effective Tools for E-Learning in Higher Education: Theory into Practice (Premier Reference Source)*. Information Science Reference. New York: Hershey.

Downes, S (2007) *What Connectivism Is*. Available online at: http://halfanhour.blogspot.co.uk/2007/02/what-connectivism-is.html [accessed 21 July 2016].

Gov.uk (2017) *School and College Funding – GOV.UK*. Available online at: https://www.gov.uk/government/policies/school-and-college-funding [accessed 10 July 2017].

Institute for Fiscal Studies (2017) *Long-Run Comparisons of Spending per Pupil Across Different Stages of Education*. London: Nuffield, pp1–22. Available online at: http://feweek.co.uk/wp-content/uploads/2017/02/IFS-Education-spending.pdf [accessed 10 July 2017].

Moules, J (2015) UK start-ups take slice of £130bn educational technology market. *Financial Times*. Available online at: https://www.ft.com/content/6e73096a-7675-11e5-933d-efcdc3c11c89?mhq5j=e3 [accessed 10 July 2017].

OECD (2015) *Students, Computers and Learning: Making the Connection.* Paris: OECD Publishing.

Ofcom (2016) *Children and Parents: Media Use and Attitudes Report.* London: Ofcom, pp1–60.

Paddick, R (2016) BYOD, is it right for your school? *Education Technology*, pp1–4. Available online at: http://edtechnology.co.uk/Article/byod-is-it-right-for-your-school [accessed 10 July 2017].

Siemens, G (2005) *Connectivism: A Learning Theory for the Digital Age.* Available online at: http://www.itdl.org/journal/jan_05/article01.htm [accessed 20 July 2016].

5
Social media literacies

What are social media?

Facebook, Twitter, Instagram et al. are all social media platforms, but what is meant by social media and why is this relevant to education?

Facebook was originally referred to as a social network. That characteristic still applies, but with a great deal more functionality. In the late 2010s, social media are means of communication that make it easy to grow networks and share multimedia content.

Who uses social media?

When Prensky (2001) coined the term *digital native*, he meant people who had grown up using computers. This was before social media and before many users of Snapchat were born. It is a common fear that excessive social media use is inhibiting traditional literacies as millennials – or those born around the millennium – are often seen hunched over their phones instead of reading books. Millennials are also known as Generation Y (coming after Gen X), social natives, Generation AO or 'always on' (Foulger, 2014), the 'IM (Instant Message) generation' (Lenhart, 2001, cited in Ingle and Duckworth, 2013), 'cyber humans', 'grasshopper minds' (Sahin, 2009, cited in Uygarer et al., 2016) and the Gamer Generation (Pedro, 2006, cited in Uygarer et al., 2016).

This chapter will unpack and critique this assumption that traditional literacies are being eroded. In doing so, we will consider the emerging literacies that are essential to understanding social media communication in the context of education. One of the drivers for this is the assumption that millennials are digitally literate (Harmes et al., 2015).

To skill or de-skill?

At the start of the new millennium, one could safely assume that young people bowing their heads towards their phones and engaging their thumbs were texting. Now, they could be studying, working on the move, business networking, outsourcing; watching video content, gambling, applying for a job; calculating, buying, selling or investing, comparing; live streaming or constructing their social persona. They will be learning that writing effective emails to your boss requires a different set of skills from making a Snapchat story for friends; networking or applying for a job on LinkedIn necessitates skills that are different from tweeting about issues. At the same time, teachers may be resistant to these skills, fearing that they de-skill (Carrington and Robinson, 2009).

From the 2010s, there was a significant multiplication of social media. Monthly Facebook users soared from 100 million in 2008 to 2 billion in 2017 (Statista, 2017). 'Digital natives', or people familiar with digital technologies (Prensky, 2001), started to integrate their media consumption with social media. Would they expect their learning to be social too? Would educators seek to limit learners' use of this phenomenon, protecting traditional learning methods? If they embraced this new personalised, anarchic web of technologies, would they have the skills and understanding to use them as a productive pedagogic tool (Noor Al-Deen and Hendricks, 2013)?

Image 5.1 New media, new literacies

Reproduced under Creative Commons Licence: **https://commons.wikimedia.org/wiki/File:Socialmedia-pm.png**

Learning by participating

Social media help people participate and can remove a feeling of being excluded. It is clear that teens at the end of the 2000s were beginning to feel empowered by the removal of many 'gatekeepers' to expression and communication: podcasting and blogging (later vlogging or video blogging) were emerging not only as part of many people's flow of information and entertainment but as a viable entry into the world of work. Indeed, as Berg (2015) revealed in *Forbes* magazine, many 'YouTubers' are now serving as powerful role models for young people entering the world of work, as they build a brand then diversify into intellectual property ownership, publishing and lucrative sponsorship deals.

Those who benefited from social media employed the skill of 'creative problem solving' (Jenkins, 2009), which is increasingly desirable in a world in which a teenager may work in an industry that does not yet exist. This book makes many references to edtech platforms helping develop the skills that are essential in the digital age: creative problem solving and self-efficacy (or the conviction that you are able to complete a task).

Real-time interaction

As educators and learners started to use collaborative tools, such as 'wikis' and alternative games, a new series of challenges was identified by Jenkins (2009): did learners have the skills to participate constructively and successfully? Furthermore, how far would academics embrace not just new technologies but new pedagogies?

Moving forward

As we move forward as educators, how can we try to understand the constantly evolving world of social media? Part of the challenge is the reality that social media literacies are hard to define and hold down because those categories and definitions are often created by users.

References

Berg, M (2015) The world's highest-paid YouTube stars 2015. *Forbes*. Available online at: https://www.forbes.com/sites/maddieberg/2015/10/14/the-worlds-highest-paid-youtube-stars-2015/#5e015a493192 [accessed 24 September 2017].

Carrington, V, Robinson, M (eds.) (2009) *Digital Literacies: Social Learning and Classroom Practices*. London: SAGE.

Foulger, M (2014) Meet the first generation of social natives. *Hootsuite Social Media Management*. Available online at: https://blog.hootsuite.com/social-natives/ [accessed 24 April 2017].

Harmes, M, Huijser H, Danaher P, Haq MU (eds.) (2015) *Myths in Learning, Teaching and Education*. London: Palgrave Publications.

Ingle, S, Duckworth, V (2013) *Enhancing Learning Through Technology in Lifelong Learning*. Maidenhead: Open University Press.

Jenkins, H (2009) *Confronting the Challenges of Participatory Culture: Media Education for the 21st Century (The John D. and Catherine T. MacArthur Foundation Reports on Digital Media and Learning)*. Cambridge, MA: MIT Press.

Noor Al-Deen, H, Hendricks, J (2013) *Social Media and Strategic Communications*. Basingstoke: Palgrave Macmillan.

Prensky, M (2001) Digital natives, digital immigrants. *On the Horizon*, 9(5): 1–6.

Statista (2017) Number of monthly active Facebook users worldwide as of 2nd quarter 2017 (in millions). *Statista*. Available online at: http://www.statista.com/statistics/264810/number-of-monthly-active-facebook-users-worldwide/ [accessed 24 September 2017].

Uygarer, R, Uzunboylu, H, Ozdamli, F (2016) *A Piece of Qualitative Study About Digital Natives*. Available online at: http://krepublishers.com/02-Journals/T-Anth/Anth-24-0-000-16-Web/Anth-24-2-000-16-Abst-PDF/T-ANTH-24-2-623-16-1489-Uygarer-R/T-ANTH-24-2-623-16-1489-Uygarer-R-Tx[27].pdf [accessed 19 August 2017].

Emerging tech

6
Artificial intelligence (AI) in education

This chapter will serve as a bridge between chapters about the broader issues and those about individual edtech platforms.

What is artificial intelligence?

Your perceptions of AI may be derived from classic science fiction films like *2001: A Space Odyssey* or TV dramas like *Humans*. The term *artificial intelligence* (AI), however, resists a single definition. The reason for this is that apps and programs often cease to be referred to as AI once they enter the mainstream (Luckin et al., 2016). Examples include computerised systems mimicking the way that humans interact by being able to recognise speech, possessing visual perception or by analysing data to determine an appropriate action and therefore a clear goal (Luckin et al., 2016).

What can artificial intelligence do for teachers and learners?

For teachers

It would be churlish to trawl through all the chapters in this book and identify examples of AI. Instead, it may be worth asking to what extent the platforms and tools in this book are evidence of the growing influence of machine learning. In addition, the remainder of this chapter will examine some AI tools that were emerging around 2016 and 2017.

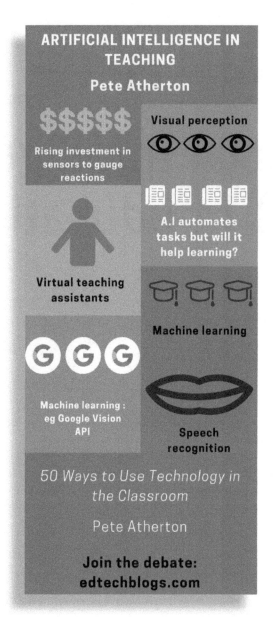

Image 6.1 Infographic: benefits of AI

Intelligent teaching assistants

The 'artificial intelligence for learning' section debates how AI teaching assistants could make stop and test assessments a thing of the past.

For learners

Could AI start to change how young people feel about their education? Many of the technologies outlined in this chapter are developing or emerging. AI, though, is already here. It may be more sensible to move on to an example of how to use an AI application, lest we engage in too much conjecture.

How to use AI: Google Vision API

The Google Vision API (or application programming interface) is an example of AI that is already here. Its face recognition and labelling functions provide glimpses into the possibilities of revolutionising the function and appearance of the classroom experience. For example, in the image of the classroom, Google Vision API has analysed the faces that are visible and attributed emotions to them.

The Vision API also creates relevant labels for image. The labels ascribed to the image of the classroom raise some pertinent questions about how classrooms are changing or may need to change.

To what extent should a classroom resemble a seminar or lecture? How does the body language of the learners resemble a meeting or training session? Should this be the case? How far should we trust this information and is there a danger that it may be mobilised to dictate unpalatable policies? Conversely, if learners are trained to determine the source and relevance of an image, this is likely to encourage self-efficacy; AI would then be there not to replace but to complement human intelligence (Luckin, 2016).

Artificial intelligence for learning

If asked about what AI means to you, it may be hard to avoid clichés, and fear-mongering stereotypes. The clichés are likely to involve robots and dystopian fears of robots replacing jobs performed by humans. Some of this fear may be amplified by the media but some of it is based on research. An example of this is PricewaterhouseCooper's report that around 30% of UK jobs would be lost to automation within 15 years (Hawksworth, 2017). The treatment of this by certain newspapers predictably inflated that figure. This estimate was lower than the 47% predicted in Frey and Osborne's (2013) study. This paper examined 702 occupations in an attempt to address John Maynard Keynes's (1933) assertion that our success in making labour more economical was outpacing the creation of new jobs (cited in Frey and Osborne, 2013).

More crucially, there are emerging issues surrounding the dizzying pace of developments in AI. To echo Barber, AI can default to measuring 'likes' or virtual affinity and rationalising administrative chores, instead of scaffolding or accelerating learning (UCL, 2017). A reason for this could be that AI has traditionally been deployed in the fields of commerce or science, rather than education (Timms, 2016, cited in Luckin et al., 2016). Given that the tech giants are investing heavily in education, could we be about to see a similar trend in AI in education? Could this be driven by the strong growth in the $460m sensor technology market (Symcox, 2017) – sensors are developing the capability to monitor engagement, enjoyment, distress and so on?

The guide in the cloud?

To test the potential of AI in education, University College London (UCL) and Pearson have started developing a virtual (not robotic) teaching assistant, called 'Colin' (Holmes et al., 2017). UCL have, of course, interrogated the various ethical implications of an AI manifestation that could potentially modify children's behaviour and replace exams with continuous assessment of pupil performance and levels of engagement (Luckin et al., 2016). Whatever the specifics, the hope is that AI like Colin could mean that teachers spend less time drawing inferences from incomplete data. That energy could be transferred to the human qualities of providing support, feedback and guidance and fostering skills like creative problem solving that are relevant to the workplace. If edtech reframes the role of the teacher from 'sage on the stage' to 'guide on the side' (Morrison, 2014), what might happen when that guide is also in the cloud?

References

Frey, C, Osborne, M (2013) *The Future of Employment: How Susceptible Are Jobs to Computerisation?* Oxford: Oxford Martin School, pp1–6. Available online at: http://www.oxfordmartin.ox.ac.uk/down loads/academic/The_Future_of_Employment.pdf [accessed 30 June 2017].

Hawksworth, R (2017) *Will Robots Steal Our Jobs? The Potential Impact of Automation on the UK and Other Major Economies 1.* London: PWC, pp1–2. Available online at: https://www.pwc.co.uk/economic-services/ukeo/pwcukeo-section-4-automation-march-2017-v2.pdf [accessed 30 June 2017].

Holmes, W, Duffy, J, Luckin, R, Forcier, L (2017) *Teacher Expertise + "Colin" = The Classroom of the Future?* London: Festival of Education.

Luckin, R (2016) Why artificial intelligence could replace exams: Professor Rose Luckin speaks on Radio 4. *Ucl.ac.uk.* Available online at: http://www.ucl.ac.uk/ioe/news-events/news-pub/ccm-news/ucl-knowledge-lab-news/why-artificial-intelligence-could-replace-exams [accessed 25 September 2017].

Luckin, R, Holmes, W, Griffiths, M, Forcier, LB (2016) *Intelligence Unleashed: An Argument for AI in Education.* London: Pearson.

Morrison, CD (2014) From 'sage on the stage' to 'guide on the side': a good start. *International Journal for the Scholarship of Teaching and Learning,* 8: 1.

Symcox, J (2017) *Sensor City Appointment to Drive High-Tech Business Growth.* Available online at: http://www.businesscloud.co.uk/news/sensor-city-appointment-to-drive-high-tech-business-growth [accessed 2 July 2017].

UCL (2017) *Why We Should Take Artificial Intelligence in Education More Seriously.* Available online at: http://www.ucl.ac.uk/ioe/news-events/news-pub/april-2016/New-paper-published-by-pearson-makes-the-case-for-why-we-must-take-artificial-intelligence-in-education-more-seriously [accessed 25 September 2017].

7
Virtual reality (VR)

What is virtual reality?

Virtual reality (VR) experiences usually involved viewing immersive visuals via a headset. These headsets can be high-end and therefore expensive, for example, the Oculus Rift. Despite their impressive design, they are likely to become obsolete. There are, however, cheaper alternatives to the VR headset, for example, VR viewers such as Google Cardboard. Like many technologies, VR has suffered a few false dawns. One of those was in the 1990s, when Nintendo launched the Virtual Boy to mass indifference: the product was withdrawn within a year (McKalin, 2014).

Where VR differs from augmented reality is in its desired total immersion of participants. Augmented reality, by contrast, allows users to remain in their own world but interact with virtual objects. Augmented reality resources can be accessed via QR codes (see Chapter 32 on QR codes) and AR codes, which resemble QR codes but with the addition of images, symbols or letters.

What can virtual reality do for teachers and learners?

For teachers

360-degree video

Learners can view 360-degree videos from YouTube through their headsets or viewers. The 'Virtual Reality' YouTube channel hosts hundreds of 360-degree videos. If you use EDpuzzle, for example, you can attach questions, either as part of or in preparation for the lesson.

For learners

VR is likely to be a welcome diversion from more traditional, conventional learning experiences. It can broaden learners' horizons by transporting them to exotic places or fire their imagination by

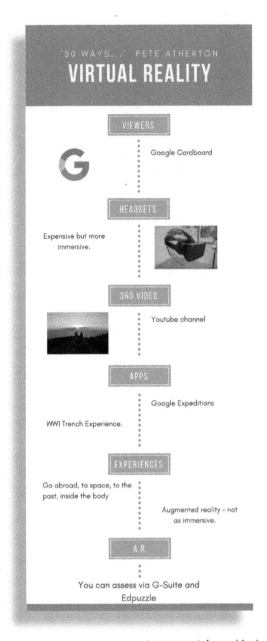

Image 7.1 Infographic: benefits of using virtual reality

immersing them in a vivid setting. If attention is a precious commodity, VR holds the golden key to access it.

How to use virtual reality

This section will suggest a shopping list and some basic instructions of how to use a selection of tools.

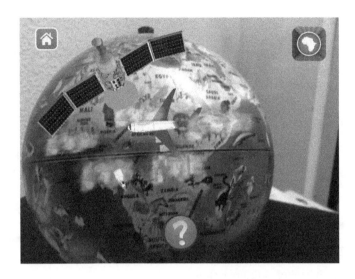

Image 7.2 Augmented reality – like reality but more so?

Google Cardboard

There are a growing number of affordable ways to view VR through headsets. 'Wearable tech' such as Google Daydream and Gear VR allows users to experience the immersion of VR by mounting their phone on a small headset. Google Cardboard's low-tech charm, though, is more pinhole camera than 360-degree camera.

Image 7.3 Google Cardboard

Once you have spent around £2 on Google Cardboard and completed the basic assembly, you will then need to search Google Play (Android devices) or the App Store (iOS devices) for VR apps that you would view with Google Cardboard attached to your mobile phone. These apps can be immersive games or 360-degree experiences of inside the human body, around the earth or in space.

Virtual reality for assessment

If your school now has G Suite (free for schools), the Expeditions app, Google Classroom, and you have invested a small amount of money in some Google Cardboard viewers, you will be able to do all of the following:

- Immerse your learners in a powerful experience.

- Ask them questions based on the content and provide real-time feedback.

- Record the marks to help plan future lessons.

Creative writing

If you are teaching war poetry and try the World War I Trench Experience app, this immersive and powerful experience can precipitate a series of questions from learners, the answers for which can be explored through the imagery in the poems. Based on both the VR experience and their analysis, they could then write a war poem of their own. The key here would be encouraging peer feedback, reflection and experimentation with imagery, vocabulary and phonology (or the sounds that words make).

English aside, creative tasks like this could also be useful for history, geography and science, technology, engineering and mathematics; indeed, all subjects would argue that immersiveness and creativity are essential components to engaging and inspiring the learners.

Spoken language

Learners could be assessed on presentations or monologues based upon their VR experience.

Virtual reality for learning

Connectivism

Perhaps one of the factors preventing many teachers from experimenting with VR is the price of the headsets. As we know, there are several solutions to this; for example, Google Cardboard. Also, it may be worth noting that, in some respects, VR can reflect the changing nature of knowledge and learning. The connectivist classroom (Siemens, 2006) is increasingly the present reality in terms of how children learn; in a learning culture like this, the mind is an ecology, a network that makes connections (Siemens, 2006, pp26–27).

Subsequently, digital cultures place greater importance on the navigation around knowledge, not the acquisition of it (Donnelly et al., 2010). Perhaps the 360-degree perspective and levels of immersion offered by VR may suit the new ways of learning more and more.

If that is the case, then VR can be part of a diverse, individualised classroom, where the teacher asks all learners to use the lesson to act on their previous feedback and goals. That might mean that the VR is only experienced by one small group at a time, hence minimising the need for pricey resources.

Links to the Teachers' Standards

S2: Promote good progress and outcomes by pupils

The VR experiences can be used as a reference point from which to connect knowledge.

S4: Impart knowledge and develop understanding through effective use of lesson time

Looking at all the sub-standards from S4, it is clear that you will be the envy of your colleagues if your activities are successful and help the pupils learn.

S5: Adapt to the strengths and needs of all pupils

The level of immersion can be an excellent way to introduce new ideas and VR can also serve as useful extension activities.

S6: Make accurate and productive use of assessment

G Suite and EDpuzzle can help assess using VR.

S8: Fulfil wider professional responsibilities

How much more enjoyable could you make your learners' experience if VR were a regular part of their learning?

References

Donnelly, R, Harvey, J, O'Rourke, K (2010) *Critical Design and Effective Tools for E-Learning in Higher Education: Theory into Practice (Premier Reference Source).* Information Science Reference. New York: Hershey.

McKalin, V (2014) Augmented reality vs. virtual reality: what are the differences and similarities? *Tech Times.* Available online at: http://www.techtimes.com/articles/5078/20140406/augmented-reality-vs-virtual-reality-what-are-the-differences-and-similarities.htm [accessed 9 July 2017].

Siemens, G (2006) *Knowing Knowledge.* Winnipeg, MB: G. Siemens, pp26–27.

Assessment/
assignment tools

8
WISEflow

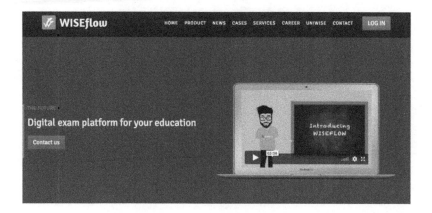

Image 8.1

The next two chapters will explore new or emerging digital assessment platforms. Firstly, we will examine WISEflow and, after that, the use of comparative judgement through a platform enticingly named No More Marking.

There are several reasons for including these two in the book. On an anecdotal note, teachers may feel that, while the delivery of content has changed and is changing swiftly, the summative assessment is lagging behind. For instance, when pupils took their GCSE exams in 2017, most of them were given exam papers, hand-wrote their answers and waited up to 3 months to receive the results. Those results will provide no evidence of how the papers were marked, though candidates can pay for remarks or a copy of their paper. This is very slow, stressful, opaque and expensive – all of which are characteristics that are at odds with digital technologies.

Could it be that the transparent feedback loops required for formative assessment are not offered for summative assessment (WISEflow, 2017)?

What is WISEflow?

WISEflow are part of a company called UNIwise. UNIwise began in 2010 as a project affiliated to the Danish Government. By 2012, it served scores of schools, colleges and universities from its base at Aarhus University. In a similar way to Turnitin, WISEflow began as exclusive to universities. Like Turnitin, WISEflow offer plagiarism detection but they also aspire to working closely with exam boards to help them provide prompt results and feedback.

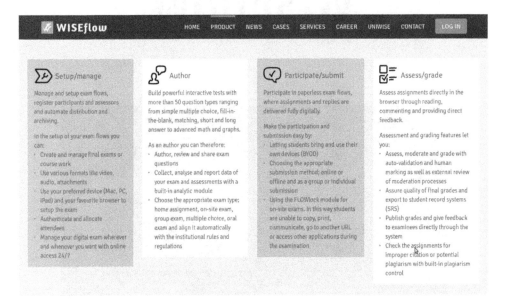

Image 8.2 WISEflow: a digital exam platform

WISEflow is a system for creating and dealing with examinations. Part of its *raison d'être* is the de-skilling of learners' hand-writing in the digital age. If students rarely write, will being forced to hand-write exams serve as a barrier to progression (Lytgens Skovfoged, 2017)?

Why digital assessment?

Here, digital assessment means the deployment of digital technologies for the creation, administration, management and feedback of examinations and tests (Gartner, 2016). In the context of higher education, digital assessment is one of the major strategic technologies. It sits comfortably in the broader context of data analytics, adaptive technologies for special educational needs and disabilities (SEND) and also a growing drive for data and outcomes to be more transparent and accountable (Gartner, 2016).

Could it be, then, that WISEflow (and their competitors) will usher in a brave new world, where candidates will no longer be hindered by their handwriting, SEND requirements, clerical error or rogue markers? There have, of course, been many scandals and errors on the part of exam boards.

Are exam boards broken?

The most recent exam board *débâcles* were the 'Hannah's sweets' question in 2015 and the errone-ous question about Tybalt in the 2017 OCR GCSE English literature paper. In the case of 'Hannah's sweets', candidates were asked an unusually challenging question. Within hours, the mainstream news media picked up on the fact that #EdexcelMaths was trending on Twitter. So difficult was the question that students expressed their distress, anger and mockery in public – to the detriment of Edexcel's and the exam system's reputations. One student parodied the question on Twitter in the following way:

> *Hannah eats some sweets. Calculate the circumference of Jupiter using your tracing paper and a rusty spoon (5 marks) #EdexcelMaths.*

(BBC News, 2015)

Should the current system of examinations pay heed to the noise of social media, even when it is not necessarily representative of the views of the student body (Sutch and Klir, 2017)?

> *What, drawn, and talk of peace? I hate the word,*
>
> *As I hate hell, all Montagues, and thee.*

(Tybalt in *Romeo and Juliet*, Act 1, scene 1)

In 2017, there certainly was an error with the GCSE English literature question on Romeo and Juliet. OCR posed the question, 'How does Shakespeare present the ways in which Tybalt's hatred of the Capulets influences the outcome of the play?' Tybalt is, of course, a Capulet himself (not a Montague) and this error led to the expected social media plague on both of OCR's houses and sig-nificant scrutiny from Ofqual, or the Office of Qualifications (Marsh, 2017). Would this error have been more likely or less likely had the exam been taken without all the heavy administration and manual labour required to make it happen?

In both cases, we see the interplay between an outdated examination system and the realities of instant communication and the attendant accountability. One of the problems that WISEflow – and No More Marking – want to fix is the way in which low-level thinking and recall are arguably rewarded by an exam system terrified of a social media backlash (Coe, 2016, cited in Busby, 2016).

References

BBC News (2015) *That* GCSE Maths Question and the Students Who Tried to Answer It. Available online at: http://www.bbc.co.uk/newsbeat/article/33022147/that-gcse-maths-question-and-the-students-who-tried-to-answer-it [accessed 26 September 2017].

Busby, E (2016) Social media fears lead to 'predictable' exam papers. *TES*, 12–13.

Gartner (2016) *Gartner Highlights Top 10 Strategic Technologies for Higher Education in 2016*. Available online at: http://www.gartner.com/newsroom/id/3225717 [accessed 14 August 2017].

Lytgens Skovfoged, S (2017) Interview in person with Steffen Lytgens Skovfoged Re: Uniwise.

Marsh, S (2017) A plague o' both your houses: error in GCSE exam paper forces apology. *The Guardian.* Available online at: https://www.theguardian.com/education/2017/may/26/error-gcse-paper-leads-to-apology-ocr-exam-board-romeo-and-juliet-tybalt-shakespeare [accessed 14 August 2017].

Sutch, T, Klir, N (2017) Tweeting about exams: investigating the use of social media over the summer 2016 session. *Research Matters: A Cambridge Assessment Publication*, 23: 2–9.

WISEflow (2017) *Brunel University London (UK) Chooses WISEflow as Platform for Digital Assessment – WISEflow*. Available online at: http://uniwise.dk/2017/08/28/brunel-university-london-uk-chooses-wiseflow-platform-digital-assessment/ [accessed 26 September 2017].

9
Comparative judgement: No More Marking

Have you ever suspected that all teachers' marking may be inaccurate and there could be a better way of doing it? Do you ever dream of a day when teachers' marking workload will actually be reduced? Especially when it comes to writing, do you feel that the current secure-fit approach to marking restricts creativity?

What is No More Marking?

The aim of No More Marking is to replace traditional marking with *comparative judgement*. This would eschew marking against a fixed rubric. To assess using comparative judgement, teachers simply place two pieces of work next to each other, then judge which one is better (NAHT, 2017). The thinking, therefore, is that student work is measured in a more sophisticated way and the judgement is absolute (Barmby, 2017). Instead of producing a summative rank order, students' work is tracked from September to June. The work can be a single piece of writing or a portfolio of artefacts.

Why No More Marking?

Teachers are acutely aware of the growing and increasingly onerous burden of marking and assessment. Furthermore, the belief is gathering momentum that conventional marking is a task that is unreliable at best and redundant at worst.

Comparative judgement may be high-tech manifestations of long-established moderation meetings but they can also provide essential continuing professional development; staff have the privilege of viewing student work from other centres.

What is the principle of comparative judgement?

The task in Image 9.1 is likely to be answered inaccurately and this proves that we are incapable of making absolute judgements.

Understanding comparative judgement

Click on the darker shade...

... and see how the scale sorts itself out ...

Image 9.1

Reproduced with permission from **https://www.nomoremarking.com/**

If we make *ordinal* judgements instead (Christodoulou, 2017a), there is a significant improvement in accuracy. To explain this point, we are much more likely to assess with accuracy if we simply judge one thing against another. For example, judging 'which shade is darker?' is easier, quicker and more likely to minimise error than 'arrange eight squares in order of darkness'.

Is this really edtech?

The reason why comparative judgement has made it into a book called *50 Ways to Use Technology Enhanced Learning in the Classroom* is because these judgements are made using an online platform called No More Marking. The scripts belonging to a number of schools are uploaded to the platform; departments will then benefit from viewing a range of centres' responses to questions and this should also reduce bias.

The selling points of comparative judgement to schools include the creation of accessible and externally verified data, quicker assessment with a lower margin of error and the opportunity to share good practice with other schools. Though the primary sector has been the most committed to the method and has the wider user base, secondary schools are now catching on to the idea. Furthermore, comparative judgement was initially applied to English in primary schools. In the secondary sector, history and modern foreign languages are also looking likely to benefit from this process, as they require pieces of extended writing.

Secondary schools: how to try out No More Marking

At the time of writing, interested parties can try it for free but would need to pay £250 + VAT to join the national judging windows (Christodoulou, 2017b) and attend a day's training. The training will take teachers through a series of tasks to enable them to develop activities that lend themselves to judging, not marking. After that, there are no further costs and participating schools will be enriched by an assessment strategy to take them from Year 10 to GCSEs.

The emphasis on formative assessment

Comparative judgement is not solely intended for summative assessment. There is a growing body of evidence and opinion that comparative judgement can raise attainment and track progress among clusters of schools that use No More Marking. The process is seen to support pupils and influence teachers' future planning, for example, an emphasis on paragraphing or composition and effect (Reynolds, 2017).

Summative assessment and convergent thinking

For several years, there was what Wheadon (2017b) termed an *agreed fiction* that levels were a realistic and fair means of summative assessment. Moreover, formative assessment has become monitored so rigidly and prescriptively that there is a blurring of the distinction between formative and summative assessment (Reynolds, 2017; Wheadon, 2017a).

In a results-driven culture with robust, perhaps punitive, levels of accountability, it could be argued that traditional marking has limited learners' ability to think.

The dominant methodology used to mark pupils' work was designed to reward *convergent* thinking (Wheadon, 2017a). How could No More Marking's algorithms detect and reward *divergent* thinking? How necessary is a more innovative form of cognition if learners are to become capable of attaining a GCSE grade 9, from the numbered grades that came into force in 2017?

References

Barmby, P (2017) Looking at progress in Year 7 English and Maths through comparative judgement. *The No More Marking Blog.* Available online at: https://blog.nomoremarking.com/looking-at-progress-in-year-7-english-and-maths-through-comparative-judgement-679d5698bf6 [accessed 3 September 2017].

Christodoulou, D (2017a) *No More Marking.* Available online at: https://www.No More Marking.com/ [accessed 5 July 2017].

Christodoulou, D (2017b) Telephone interview with Daisy Christodoulou for *50 Ways to Use Technology Enhanced Learning in the Classroom.*

NAHT (2017) *Teacher Assessment of Writing: Remove "Secure Fit" and Change the Teacher Assessment Frameworks.* Available online at: http://www.naht.org.uk/welcome/news-and-media/key-topics/assessment/teacher-assessment-of-writing-remove-secure-fit-and-change-frameworks/ [accessed 16 August 2017].

Reynolds, J (2017) Bursting the bubble: managing clusters with comparative judgement. *The No More Marking Blog*. Available online at: https://blog.No More Marking.com/managing-clusters-with-com parative-judgement-7a4df2e4a960 [accessed 6 July 2017].

Wheadon, C (2017a) Measuring progress towards GCSE English. *The No More Marking Blog*. Available online at: https://blog.No More Marking.com/measuring-progress-towards-gcse-english-8ed4006c025e [accessed 5 July 2017].

Wheadon, C (2017b) Telephone interview with Chris Wheadon for *50 Ways to Use Technology Enhanced Learning in the Classroom*.

10
Spiral

What is Spiral?

Spiral.ac is a formative assessment platform. Where it differs from some of its competitors, for example Goformative and Nearpod, is in its more acute awareness of the importance of pedagogy. Joining is free and there is no download. Image 10.1 summarises the other pricing options.

Image 10.1 Homepage of Spiral.ac

What can Spiral do for teachers and learners?

For teachers

The main appeal of Spiral will, of course, be its simplicity. Teachers will find it easy to import classes, ask questions and ensure that all learners are involved. The Quickfire and Discuss features are accessible ways to practise questioning techniques, for example assertive questioning, or assess prior knowledge (Petty, 2004). In case you are unsure about how to implement what you know about formative assessment, Spiral offers a helping hand. Spiral has partly been conceived with theories about assessment for learning in mind. An example of this is the notion that Spiral can help use the work produced to adapt the teaching and, ensuingly, help meet learner needs (Black and Wiliam, 2010).

Image 10.2 Infographic: benefits of using Spiral

For learners

The screenshot below summarises the appeal of Spiral for learners. From left to right, the first benefit is the way that Spiral encourages learners to feel that they can receive speedy feedback on their answers and have the chance to improve. This could remove some of the pressure on learners to be right and help create a more harmonious learning environment.

Spiral Pricing

Image 10.3

The symbol in the middle stresses engagement. How likely is it that learners will feel valued by the fact that all learners are expected to be active at all times? This could improve the culture of the class, as it could clarify that it is not acceptable for only the same small number of learners to contribute.

Finally, collaboration. Spiral see collaboration as stretching and challenging by sharing model answers, transferring the responsibility for scaffolding from the teacher to the whole class and ensuring that there are no passengers.

How to use Spiral

A class join a Spiral session by visiting gospiral.ac, then entering a code. The code is created when the teacher logs in.

Aside from this, most of the information on how to use Spiral is conveyed in a series of very simple videos on this page (see Image 10.4).

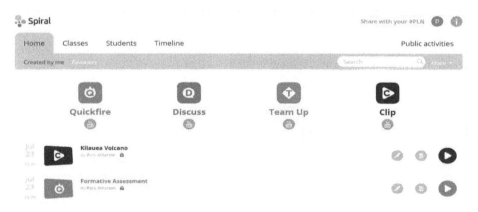

Image 10.4 Simple video tutorials – thank you, Spiral!

Spiral for assessment

There are several collaborative apps that are likely to be both engaging and educational: Quickfire, Discuss, Team Up and Clip. All of them wear their pedagogic intentions on their sleeves, especially in terms of ways to assess, provide feedback and use data.

Clip resembles EDpuzzle in the way that teachers can source videos from YouTube and add questions to them. Where it is different from EDpuzzle is that learners can add comments in a live feed while the video is playing. Discuss is an interactive presentation tool. It is accessed by way of learners entering a code. When they are 'in', they can answer multiple-choice or in-depth questions posed by the teacher.

Team Up

If you ask small groups of learners to make a collaborative presentation, the teacher could track the contribution of each student.

Quickfire

This feature is akin to an online poll. It is intended as a swift formative assessment tool.

You can read more on Spiral and formative assessment here: **https://spiral.ac/support/formative-assessment**

Spiral for learning

Can an edtech platform like Spiral be a catalyst for clearer formative assessment? If that is the case, the assessment data it produces could enable teachers to focus on the qualities of students' work and what they need to do to improve. Is it not the case that the progress reports generated by Spiral (and other edtech platforms) may purport to encourage reflection but could contribute to learner anxiety and a preoccupation with the 'right' answers (Black and Wiliam, 2010)? Teachers may need to balance the extensive empirical data that they will have on the learners with the fact that they are helping develop human beings.

To challenge this, the allusion to 'growth mindset' on the website builds a helpful bridge between the teachers, the tech and the learners. The various tools and activities on Spiral offer a helping hand to teachers to guide the fragile minds in front of them from negative internal monologues to a focus on learning and measuring improvement (Dweck, 2012).

Links to the Teachers' Standards

S1: Set high expectations which inspire, motivate and challenge pupils

Creating a challenging environment is more likely if learners feel valued and supported. Spiral intends to create this culture.

S2: Promote good progress and outcomes by pupils

The many ways that learners can reflect on their progress is likely to help them understand how they learn.

S3: Demonstrate good subject and curriculum knowledge

The responsibility of addressing misunderstandings can be shared with the whole group.

S4: Plan and teach well-structured lessons

There are several immersive and stimulating activities for students; for example, videos that pause for the students to answer a variety of question types.

S5: Adapt to the strengths and needs of all pupils

Spiral offers variations in question type, feedback type, activity and pace.

S6: Make accurate and productive use of assessment

The best way that Spiral can help you meet this Standard is by enabling the learners to respond to feedback.

S8: Fulfil wider professional responsibilities

To what extent could you use Spiral to have a positive influence over formative assessment in your school?

References

Black, P, Wiliam, D (2010) Inside the black box: raising standards through classroom assessment. *Phi Delta Kappan*, 92(1): 81–90.

Dweck, C (2012) *Mindset*. London: Robinson.

Petty, G (2004) *Evidence Based Teaching: A Practical Approach*. Cheltenham: Nelson Thornes.

11
Goformative

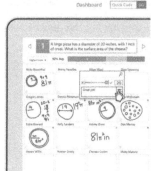

Image 11.1 Why wait for feedback when you can provide it now?

What is Goformative?

Goformative is an online formative assessment tool. The flow chart on Goformative's homepage delineates its simplicity. To use Goformative, teachers create an assignment, assign that assignment to their learners, view results in real time and then provide feedback. In terms of monitoring learner progress, the platform can generate 'live results' and allow teachers to intervene at the most opportune moments.

What can Goformative do for teachers and learners?

For teachers

Given Ofsted's renewed emphasis on assessment for learning and the need to check understanding frequently, this tool could be a welcome shortcut in a cluttered edtech landscape.

The Goformative dashboard provides templates like the one below. These ready-made activities can save time on planning, as resources can be easily adapted. If piles of books and files exacerbate your workload, Goformative offers the possibility that teaching and learning may be administered paperlessly.

Pete Atherton
50 Ways to Use Technology in the Classroom

GOFORMATIVE

UNCLUTTERED INTERFACE
No wasting time trying to figure it out

EASY FOR TEACHERS
Great for technophobes

REAL-TIME FEEDBACK
Why wait until the teacher has ploughed their way through a pile of marking?

VARIED ASSESSMENT
Includes pre-made assignments

GO PAPERLESS
Save money, save the planet. What's not to like?

MANY WAYS TO JOIN A CLASS
Google Apps, Clever, a code, Excel

SAGE PUBLICATIONS
JOIN THE DEBATE: EDTECHBLOGS.COM

Image 11.2 Infographic: benefits of using Goformative

For learners

Goformative is compatible with smartphones and tablets, which may be appealing to learners who prefer to be attached to their own devices. At any key stage, it can be preferable to receive feedback in real time, instead of having to wait until their teacher has conquered a mountain of marking.

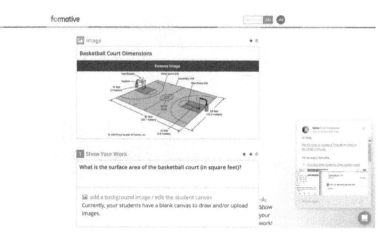

Image 11.3 Goformative sample formative assessment

There are several ways for learners to show their work: they can type or draw using the mouse or straight on to the screen of a tablet. They can also add images and illustrate and add to their answers. Doing this can help scaffold tasks for less able learners but it can also stretch and challenge higher achievers, as they use the visual image to show their creative flair or sophisticated understanding.

How to use Goformative

Create a new class

To create a new class, simply click on the relevant bar and give your class a name. You can then generate a code, which will later be shared with your class.

Enrol the learners into your class

There are five ways to enrol learners into a class (at the time of writing).

Through Google Apps

The learners will need to click on the following URL: goformative.com/#signup. They will then be prompted to 'sign up with Google'. From there, the teacher will display their class code, which will then be entered by each learner.

Through Clever

The school IT department or administrator may have a portal link. If they do, they could sign in through Clever and enter the class code provided by the teacher.

By importing an existing group into my Goformative class

To do this, you simply add your class to an Excel file and email it to: hello@goformative.com. If you include your class code, it should be active within 24 hours.

Independently

If students want to join the class in their own way, they simply sign up at goformative.com/#signup, then enter the aforementioned class code.

Through mass enrolment

If the whole school want to be involved, you can email them and request this from hello@goformative.com.

Goformative for assessment

Goformative provide some ready-made assignments, for example, *Checks for Understanding*. These templates can ask learners to describe three things that they learned in class today, how the lesson could be used in the real world, a self-evaluation and even how they might have taught today's lesson if they were the teacher. The final pre-made assignment could help stretch and challenge learners by asking them what they would like to learn more about, which would then prompt some independent research, a group project or an extension task.

Goformative for learning

The Goformative community

Joining this virtual community can connect like-minded educators whose images are presented in a gallery alongside their Twitter handle. If you wish to take your support of Goformative to the next level, there is also the option of applying for an 'awesome' educator badge. To qualify for this, you could write for the Formative blog or create collaborative formatives.

In common with many edtech providers, Goformative aims to cultivate brand advocates. Brand advocates for edtech platforms are typically unpaid superfans whose belief in a brand influences them to promote it to their students and peers and through social media (Sussman, 2015). Similarly, Kahoot! have 'Kahoot! Evangelists', who are essentially doing the same thing but with a little more passion (Brooker, 2016).

In a communication landscape increasingly led by social media, it is advocacy, not advertising, that is likely to produce effective and low-risk results (Fuggetta, 2012). As edtech continues to flourish, however, how long can the providers expect busy professionals essentially to work for them for nothing?

Links to the Teachers' Standards

S1: Set high expectations which inspire, motivate and challenge pupils

Goformative's 'Show your work' function encourages stretch and challenge by providing opportunities for extension activities. The questions can be as high-order as is appropriate for the learners.

S2: Promote good progress and outcomes by pupils

Goformative's autograding provides swift and simple formative grades for all learners.

The 'live results' page enables teachers to give instant feedback and for pupils to act on this feedback.

S5: Adapt to the strengths and needs of all pupils

The short answers, true or false and multiple-choice questions can be used to scaffold content, whilst the 'show your work' questions can be high-order.

S6: Make accurate and productive use of assessment

Goformative can display all pupils' answers to the teacher, or, if appropriate, to the entire class. Learners will therefore be given both formative feedback and summative scores.

Goformative's 'Live results' will highlight the successes and areas for improvement.

This could be particularly effective through a 'flipped classroom', where learners will have completed tasks online but the lesson time will be spent acting on the written feedback and receiving further oral feedback from the teacher.

References

Brooker, J (2016) *Kahoot and Formative Assessment.* Interview conducted over Skype, 19 August.

Fuggetta, R (2012) *Brand Advocates.* Hoboken, NJ: Wiley.

Sussman, B (2015) *Influencers vs. Ambassadors vs. Advocates: Stop the Confusion!* Entrepreneur. Available online at: https://www.entrepreneur.com/article/249947 [accessed 3 April 2017].

12
A Tale Unfolds

Image 12.1

What is A Tale Unfolds?

A Tale Unfolds makes video-based stimulus materials and teaching packs that use digital literacy to improve 'traditional' literacy radically (Traynor, 2017). These traditional literacies involve writing in several forms: tasks could require pupils to create an interactive book, write a news report or script a film trailer. A Tale Unfolds is largely concerned with Key Stages 1 and 2. Though this book is prioritising Key Stages 3–5, there are resources designed to bridge the gap between Years 6 and 7. In that respect, A Tale Unfolds could be a welcome addition to intervention strategies for Year 7 pupils whose literacy levels need to improve.

Image 12.2 Infographic: benefits of using A Tale Unfolds

What can A Tale Unfolds do for teachers and learners?

For teachers

Many teachers would be seduced by the thought of acquiring up to 30 hours of engaging lesson plans that scaffold the necessary digital skills and develop literacy. Furthermore, the testimonials and data sets on the website emphasise how they use digital technologies to inspire pupils to read and write. The feedback on pupil engagement has been highly positive; for example, that pupils have been happier to complete sentence-level work after completing the tasks from the resource pack.

One of the starting points for A Tale Unfolds is a perceived disconnect between literacy requirements and engagement with technology (Traynor, 2017).

For learners

Engagement

The intention is that teachers don't stand in the way of the learners and that accords them greater autonomy (Traynor, 2017). The tasks also require a great deal of creativity.

Literacy skills

Each lesson contains a detailed writing task, which is initially modelled by the teacher. The resource packs require analytical reading, spoken language and presenting.

Presentation/social and employability skills

The idea of filming an amalgamation of written stories can help pupils' presentation skills. Working collaboratively to complete a complicated film production improves social skills. In terms of employability, pupils will also require digital and traditional literacies to complement their competency in conversing, co-operating and presenting.

How to use A Tale Unfolds

This section has selected the resource that is relevant to both Key Stage 2 and Year 7.

War Story

The War Story project is a resource pack which comprises a film trailer and animation as stimulus materials and a series of writing tasks; for example, describing characters and settings and narrative writing. Other writing tasks in the pack include detective reports and a diary entry from a character. Much of the writing work is modelled by the teacher.

The project culminates in a film production, either in groups or as a whole class. A Tale Unfolds provides extensive support on pre-production, filming and editing techniques.

A Tale Unfolds for assessment

The activities and resource packs are often used as interventions for Year 7 learners who have fallen behind on their literacy and are struggling to cope with the transition to secondary standards (Traynor, 2017).

One of the assessment methods that A Tale Unfolds is exploring is the notion of replacing traditional marking with making comparative judgement (Traynor, 2017). This thinking draws on the work of Wheadon (2016), whose No More Marking method is deconstructed in Chapter 9.

A Tale Unfolds for learning

Indeed, since the start of what is now referred to as the digital age, there have been some enduring contradictions (Atherton, 2017). For instance, does edtech technology enhanced learning always enhance learning, and why should there be a separation between edtech and traditional learning (Atherton, 2017; Traynor, 2017)?

In the digital age, learners and their teachers are trying to understand new literacies and ways of learning. As digital natives beget social natives (Prensky, 2001, 2012; Foulger, 2014), one of the challenges is for edtech platforms to help pupils understand how digital content is made. In doing so, they are more likely to be discerning creators of content, not just passive consumers (Traynor, 2017).

Encouraging activism

A Tale Unfolds' resources are designed to empower children to find their own voice.

An example of this strategy can be found in the youth vote and 'Pupil Prime Minister' packs. Improvements in literacy, of course, are essential components in this desire to empower.

Links to the Teachers' Standards

S1: Set high expectations which inspire, motivate and challenge pupils

Activities necessitate careful planning and support.

S2: Promote good progress and outcomes by pupils

A Tale Unfolds encourages pride and confidence.

S4: Plan and teach well-structured lessons

The lessons are planned for you.

S5: Adapt to the strengths and needs of all pupils

Think of Year 7s who have fallen behind on their literacy.

S6: Make accurate and productive use of assessment

Useful for Year 7 interventions.

S8: Fulfil wider professional responsibilities

The work can be celebrated and showcased.

References

Atherton, P (2017) *Kahoot for Assessment*. Liverpool: Kindle. Available online at: https://www.amazon.co.uk/Using-Kahoot-Assessment-teachers-learners-ebook/dp/B071CJSTC4/ref=sr_1_1?ie=UTF8&qid=1492696884&sr=8-1&keywords=pete+atherton [accessed 20 April 2017].

Foulger, M (2014) Meet the first generation of social natives. *Hootsuite Social Media Management,* Web 24 April 2017.

Prensky, M (2001) Digital natives, digital immigrants. *On the Horizon*, 9(5): 1–6.

Prensky, M (2012) *From Digital Natives to Digital Wisdom*. London: SAGE.

Traynor, D (2017) *Interview about A Tale Unfolds* (over the telephone).

Wheadon (2016) Improving critical reading through comparative judgement – David Didau: the learning spy. *David Didau: The Learning Spy*. Available online at: http://www.learningspy.co.uk/english-gcse/critical-reading/ [accessed 4 October 2017].

13
Book Creator

What is Book Creator?

Image 13.1 Would you like to see your learners on this page?

Book Creator is an ebook creation tool. It provides templates to enable anyone not only to make an ebook but also to publish it to Apple's iBooks store. If everyone has a book in them, Book Creator could help unleash a great deal of untapped potential, from a short, in-class activity to a fully formed eportfolio or self-published novel. As of August 2017, Book Creator was available on PC or laptop or as an app for Android or iOS devices. A free plan allows one library of up to 40 books.

What can Book Creator do for teachers and learners?

For teachers

Multimedia teaching resources and incorporating other apps

Your teaching materials can be made much more attractive through this tool. To take this further, more tech-savvy teachers may want to experiment with pulling content from other apps into Book Creator, for example, Explain Everything, iMovie and Popplet.

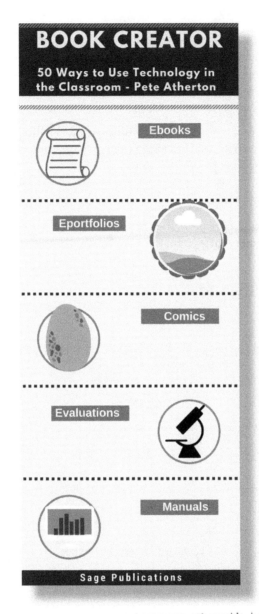

Image 13.2 Infographic: benefits of using Book Creator

Share memories

After a trip, visit or event, you could collect the photographs and make them into an engaging comic or book, with music and narration.

Model finished products

One example of how you could use Book Creator for teacher modelling would be to show an example of a completed write-up of a science experiment or a book of interactive stories.

For learners

There are many routes that learners can take on Book Creator in order to express themselves in a way that suits their passions and aspirations. They could create a realistic comic, a digital portfolio of their research or creative work; they could make travelogues or use Book Creator to show how they solved a mathematics or science problem.

Learners could work alone or in collaboration with their peers, either locally or globally. Though this could be a rewarding activity, teachers would need to make learners aware of the implications in terms of copyright and assessment.

Learning about employment

Though learners are unlikely to make money from their ebooks, they can at least learn about the importance of dissemination of their creativity.

How to use Book Creator

Photos

Tap the + icon on a tablet and click on a PC/laptop/Chromebook, then add photos stored on your device or from a cloud.

Camera

The same process enables you to add your own photos.

Pen

On a tablet, you can draw with an iPad pen; on a PC, you can click and drag to draw words and pictures.

Text

Click or tap the 'T' icon to display a keyboard on which to type.

Sound

Selecting this allows you to record your voice (or other sounds) or add music.

Book Creator also lets users add videos and shapes to their ebooks or other creations.

Book Creator for assessment

High-order thinking

Bloom's digital taxonomy (Anderson and Krathwohl, 2001, cited in Churches, 2008) places 'creating' at the highest point on its pyramid. Here, creating can incorporate directing, publishing, remixing and podcasting (Churches, 2008). The significance of this is discussed in the 'Book Creator for Learning' section. However we interpret – or respect – this notion, it is clear that the digital age presents a plethora of opportunities for teachers to assess creative tasks.

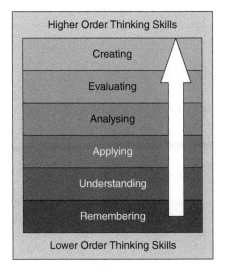

Image 13.3

Image reproduced via Wikicommons licence: **https://upload.wikimedia.org/wikipedia/commons/2/29/Bloom%27s_Taxonomy.png**

At the highest level of teacher confidence, you may want to consider incorporating a formative assessment app such as Spiral or Goformative. This could help you close the gap between learners' prior knowledge, their current progress and where they need to be (Hattie, 2008).

Book Creator for learning

Creativity and high-order thinking

Anderson and Krathwohl's (2001) 'digital taxonomy' was intended to reflect the changing nature of teaching and learning in the digital age (cited in Churches, 2008). This assumes that learners cannot create unless they have already demonstrated that they have remembered, understood, applied, analysed and evaluated. It could be argued that this thinking fails to recognise the often prodigious talents of learners with dyslexia or autism, for whom understanding can sometimes be hampered by cognitive impairment. Perhaps the most sensible way to consider Bloom's digital taxonomy is with the proviso that it is not necessarily a linear process, nor should it be approached as such. Additionally, educators need to be mindful of the fact that both the edtech landscape and digital cultures have undergone considerable change since the publication of these papers. Is it time, then, to deploy tools like Book Creator to help usher in a truly progressive learning environment?

The danger, of course, is that new and emerging edtech can be merely absorbed into existing practices and serve as an expensive typewriter, worksheet or overhead projector (Holland, 2017). When the 'grammar' of education stays the same, the new technology cannot infiltrate (Cuban, 2017). For the technology to be truly transformational, it must help change the teaching methods and what students learned. None of this is likely without a clear policy and a set of goals (Cuban, 2017).

Links to the Teachers' Standards

S1: Set high expectations which inspire, motivate and challenge pupils

The ability to create multiple redrafts and to explore creativity with time, a showcase and significant support could help stretch and challenge.

S2: Promote good progress and outcomes by pupils

Book Creator provides scope for learners to build confidence and take pride in their work. They could ultimately produce a piece of content that gains worldwide recognition.

S3: Demonstrate good subject and curriculum knowledge

Teachers, of course, could publish their own resources for the world to see. This could be a way to position them as an expert in their field.

S4: Plan and teach well-structured lessons

Book Creator provides a laudable range of ways to create pacey and stimulating learning episodes.

S5: Adapt to the strengths and needs of all pupils

The planning, learning goals, medium of communication and feedback can all be carefully differentiated. Consider, for example, the scaffolding that learners would need if creating a book of poems or stories. How could you also cater for learners with an insatiable appetite for learning?

S6: Make accurate and productive use of assessment

You can import formative assessment apps like Classkick and Nearpod. As learners can work collaboratively, they could also provide peer feedback.

S8: Fulfil wider professional responsibilities

Book Creator can help promote your institution through celebrating the learners' creations. You could even create Oscars or Booker Prize-style awards ceremonies for the best work in each category.

References

Churches, A (2008) *Bloom's Digital Taxonomy*. PB Works. Available online at: http://burtonslife learning.pbworks.com/f/BloomDigitalTaxonomy2001.pdf [accessed 24 July 2017].

Cuban, L (2017) *Change and Stability in Classrooms, Schools, and Districts (Part 2)*. Available online at: https://larrycuban.wordpress.com/2017/05/30/change-and-stability-in-classrooms-schools-and-districts-part-2/ [accessed 19 June 2017].

Hattie, J (2008) *Visible Learning*. London: Routledge.

Holland, B (2017) *The Power of Paradigms to Transform Education*. Education Week – EdTech Researcher. Available online at: http://blogs.edweek.org/edweek/edtechresearcher/2017/06/the_power_of_paradigms_to_transform_education.html [accessed 19 June 2017].

14
VoiceThread

What is VoiceThread?

VoiceThread is a media player that resembles a slideshow but is much more collaborative and diverse than that. The slideshow element is augmented by a discussion space, so that any presentation is truly interactive. Its target market ranges from kindergarten to secondary school, higher education and business. VoiceThread's offer is to enable *conversations in the cloud* about multimedia content. Learners are able to present through and interact with images, video, audio and so on.

What can VoiceThread do for teachers and learners?

For teachers

VoiceThread is free for a single educator and up to 50 student accounts, all of which you can access.

Custom homepage

All your VoiceThread content can be organised on one convenient web page. This web page can be embedded on to the virtual learning environment or other learning management system.

Pedagogy

If you are aware that presentations are often teacher-centred, you can ensure that you embed more participatory, engaging methods into your lessons and flipped learning activities.

Security

The fact that VoiceThread stores data in a cloud can be appealing, as it removes the need to store everything on a sometimes slow or limited school server. Teachers may fear being hacked or losing files; VoiceThread offer reassurance about the security of their data centres and infrastructure. The security settings also ensure that the general public cannot access students' work.

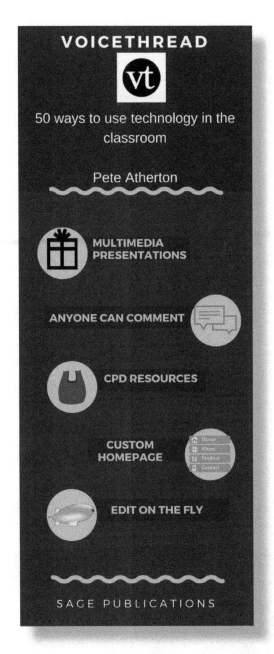

Image 14.1 Infographic: benefits of using VoiceThread

Continuing professional development

VoiceThread hosts regular workshops to help with lesson planning and how to get the best out of the platform.

For learners

VoiceThread is device-agnostic and accessible. The teacher can set up a student account without the need to supply an email address. The lessons are likely to be engaging, as there are multiple opportunities for learner input. Indeed, if learners thrive by working collaboratively, they can construct multimedia slideshows together.

How to use VoiceThread

The starting point is uploading a file from your computer, taking a photo or recording a video from your webcam. You could also access files from a URL, Flickr, Google Drive, the New York Public Library or the Khan Academy.

The completed file can be shared as a link, an embed code; you can then decide whether you want the file to be secure, completely public, even editable by anyone. If you are allowing comments from all users, you can moderate these by rolling over the image of the person who has made the comment and clicking the 'eyelid' button to open it up for all to see and hear. If you want to prioritise your learners' contributions, you can reorder the comments by dragging and dropping them.

Doodling

This function is designed to maximise engagement. In short, you can draw on any slide to highlight specific features or make connections. PC users can do this by clicking and dragging the mouse or tablet or interactive whiteboard users can draw with their fingers or a stylus pen.

VoiceThread for assessment

Flipped learning

The image below shows how the teacher can play a multimedia slideshow and ask the class questions. The left sidebar shows the names of the learners, here depicted as a series of crude self-portraits.

Image 14.2 Listen to each learner's responses

Clicking or tapping the image of each learner plays their audio response and provides evidence of their progress, which can be assessed.

Peer feedback

Learners can add voice or text comments to each other's work to provide peer feedback. Group tasks could be accompanied by audio commentaries summarising each learner's role; this will make the work easier to assess.

VoiceThread for learning

There are several academic papers exploring the effects of using VoiceThread in a variety of contexts. Some are more relevant to the context of adult learners and hence are not part of this book (Delmas, 2017).

Also, and somewhat problematically, some of the literature cited on the VoiceThread website refers to theories linking learning to the human brain. One of these is Medina (2014), who claimed that learning in *multisensory environments* is more powerful and enduring than that experienced in *unisensory environments* (Medina, 2014). VoiceThread clearly encourages multisensory experiences, such as the recording of audio, kinetic acts like drawing, viewing video and typing text. Whether these lead to quicker, more permanent learning is a moot point.

What we can always fall back on are notions that are not restricted to the cognitive domain, such as Kingsley's (2015) study on using VoiceThread to develop high-order thinking through the writing of book reviews. Here, adequate scaffolding was provided via a graphic organiser which led learners from remembering to defending, recommending and critiquing, then finally creating. VoiceThread would combine self-efficacy with sophisticated thinking as learners would become multimodal designers as they used multimedia slides to construct their reviews (Dalton, 2015, cited in Kingsley, 2015, p42).

Links to the Teachers' Standards

S1: Set high expectations which inspire, motivate and challenge pupils

You can allow learners to plan challenging, self-directed tasks that offer various ways of expressing themselves.

S2: Promote good progress and outcomes by pupils

You can build on prior knowledge and offer feedback in a variety of forms.

S3: Demonstrate good subject and curriculum knowledge

The multimodal literacies required for memorable VoiceThreads will allow you to indulge in deep subject knowledge.

(Continued)

(Continued)

S4: Plan and teach well-structured lessons

The variety of tasks should make lessons more varied and engaging.

S5: Adapt to the strengths and needs of all pupils

Differentiation is facilitated by the choice of actions on VoiceThread.

S6: Make accurate and productive use of assessment

Formative assessment here can take many forms: text, voice, video, drawing and links to multimedia content.

S7: Manage behaviour effectively to ensure a good and safe environment

The visibility of each learner alongside the teacher's VoiceThread encourages accountability and self-efficacy.

References

Delmas, P (2017) Using VoiceThread to create community in online learning. *TechTrends*. Available online at: https://link.springer.com/article/10.1007/s11528-017-0195-z#main-content [accessed 4 October 2017].

Kingsley, T (2015) *Indiana Reading Journal Volume 44 Issue 1. Joomag*. Available online at: https://view.joomag.com/indiana-reading-journal-volume-44-issue-1/0804259001441217311/p36? [accessed 25 July 2017].

Medina, J (2014) *Brain Rules*. Seattle, WA: Pear Press.

15
AnswerGarden

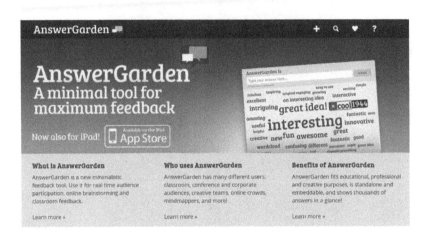

Image 15.1

What is AnswerGarden?

AnswerGarden.ch is described on the website as a feedback tool and defines itself by its minimalism. It creates 'social word clouds' from every set of answers, so the class can clearly see the most popular answer, though not necessarily the most correct. In many ways, it is a hybrid of collaborative display boards like Padlet and word cloud tools like Wordle or Tag Cloud. AnswerGarden can be enjoyed on PC or as a tablet app.

What can AnswerGarden do for teachers and learners?

For teachers

Icebreakers

In similar ways to polling tools, teachers can use the word cloud generated by AnswerGarden to help people to learn about each other. You could ask a question, for example, 'what is your favourite colour?', then try and group people with the most or least similar preferences.

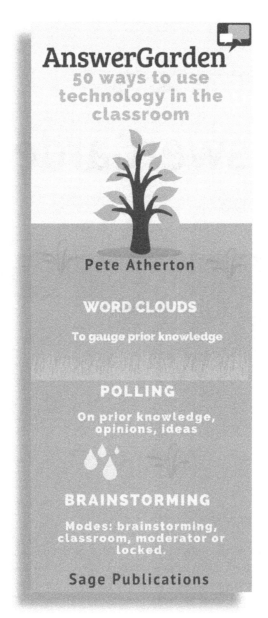

Image 15.2 Infographic: benefits of using AnswerGarden

AnswerGarden could also be used for diagnostic tests or quick revision sessions.

For learners

Brainstorming anonymously

When all contributions are anonymous, no idea is irrelevant and no voice is louder than another's. That is the somewhat halcyon view of employing tools such as these.

Collaboration

AnswerGarden can be used like Padlet for brainstorming but can also mirror polling or feedback tools like Poll Everywhere or Slido. As with all of the tools selected for this book, it has potential for offering meaningful feedback and could facilitate formative dialogue between teachers and learners.

Concise answers

AnswerGarden can restrict answers to 20 or 40 characters. This could help pairs of learners think carefully about their contributions.

How to use AnswerGarden

Create

Creating a new AnswerGarden forms a new URL (or web address). The learners simply join by entering the URL. The URL could be accessed via a QR code, so they do not have to enter a URL manually.

Modes: brainstorm, moderator, classroom and locked

In 'brainstorm mode' the word cloud will be populated by each and every contribution, however appropriate or accurate. If the lesson activity looks in danger of spinning out of control, the session can enter 'locked' mode, which closes the session to new answers. 'Moderator mode' offers some form of buffer between low quality or disruptive answers. 'Classroom mode' means that the same answer can only be submitted once, which means that the brainstorming session would no longer be about popularity or being correct.

Ask a question or examine a statement by typing it in the search box. You can share it with your class, with parents or colleagues. The question can also be intended to solicit a potentially crowdsourced answer, perhaps embedded on a website, blog or virtual learning environment, such as Canvas.

Submit

Participants submit their answers and they start to flourish in the 'AnswerGarden', as it were.

AnswerGarden for assessment

Differentiation

If you trust your learners to be transparent about their answers, the word clouds produced on AnswerGarden could be skilful ways of differentiating your lessons. Before the questions have been asked, you may want to organise your small groups by placing similar abilities together, mixing high and low attainers, sitting English as an additional language (EAL) learners together for mutual support or mixing with high achievers for challenge (as being EAL has no connection with academic ability).

After the answers have been given, you could ask the learners to create a rank order of answers in terms of accuracy and complexity. These categories could be informed by grading criteria, Bloom's taxonomy or by your own criteria.

AnswerGarden for learning

Divergent thinking

Teachers can utilise AnswerGarden's word clouds to promote creativity and problem solving. One of the enduring themes of this book is the necessary coexistence of online and offline learning. With that in mind, teachers could use the word clouds as a lotus blossom exercise. This kind of activity asks participants to brainstorm as normal, then create a new 'lotus blossom' for a selection of its petals. For example, if learners were asked to brainstorm the themes in *Romeo and Juliet* and one of these themes was 'fate', they would then create a new lotus blossom all about fate (Fisher and Frey, 2014).

On its own, AnswerGarden would not precipitate the learners' full potential for divergent thinking. Combined with the offline tasks, AnswerGarden could serve as a springboard towards the growing notion that exams reward convergent thinking, when it is divergent thinking that helps secure the highest grades (Christodoulou, 2017; Wheadon, 2017).

Links to the Teachers' Standards

S1: Stretch and challenge

The word clouds produced by brainstorming sessions can encourage the high-order thinking required to make connections between ideas, concepts or facts.

S2: Promote good progress and outcomes by pupils

One of the essential functions of online polls is to gauge prior knowledge and diagnose strengths and areas needing support.

S4: Plan and teach well-structured lessons

The key to using AnswerGarden to help improve the pace and structure of the lessons is to build the knowledge, the thinking, the application and the mastery. You could return to AnswerGarden at the end of the lesson or the following day.

S5: Adapt to the strengths and needs of all pupils

What the class do with the word clouds can create a necessary layer of scaffolding or a deeper level of challenge.

S6: Make accurate and productive use of assessment

AnswerGarden helps test prior knowledge and diagnose gaps or misconceptions.

S7: Manage behaviour effectively to ensure a good and safe environment

AnswerGarden's settings can hide or filter out inappropriate responses.

References

Christodoulou, D (2017) *No More Marking*. Available online at: https://www.nomoremarking.com/ [accessed 5 July 2017].

Fisher, D, Frey, N (2014) *Checking for Understanding*. Alexandria, VA: ASCD.

Wheadon, C (2017) Measuring progress towards GCSE English. *The No More Marking Blog*. Available online at: https://blog.nomoremarking.com/measuring-progress-towards-gcse-english-8ed4006c025e [accessed 5 July 2017].

16

Nearpod

What is Nearpod?

LIke Classkick, Goformative, Edmodo and Spiral, Nearpod is a teaching and learning app that bestows on learners the gift of varied, interactive lessons and real-time feedback.

What can Nearpod do for teachers and learners?

For teachers

Time-poor teachers may be attracted to the idea that the Nearpod app can function as a user-friendly hub for some or all of their lessons. You may, however, want to think very carefully about the wholesale adoption of any app or tool.

Free lessons

Nearpod stores hundreds of paid-for lessons but you can also restrict your search to free content. It is essential to trial your lessons prior to unleashing them on your classes: non-American learners could be alienated by some of the language and content. The real pleasure will be in using Nearpod to plan your own lessons. There are many gratifying touches to add a little finesse or memorability to your activities. Examples of these include the ability to add GIFs to your slides, simply by entering the desired term into a Google-powered search box.

Reports

Your classes are able to join a session *en masse* and Nearpod provides reports on their engagement and activity. This will be evaluated in the section on assessment.

For learners

Varied activities

Variety is clearly built into Nearpod's design. During a typical Nearpod-enabled lesson, learners could have quizzes, take part in polls and draw their answers; they could also go on a virtual field trip, where they can view 360-degree video through a virtual reality viewer or headset.

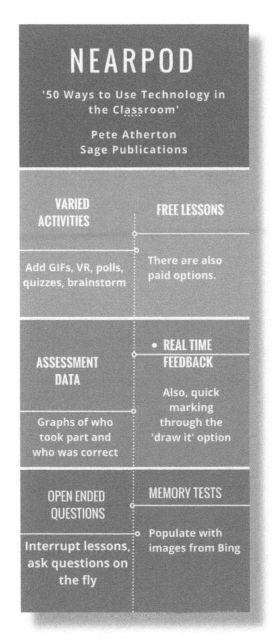

Image 16.1 Infographic: benefits of using Nearpod

How to use Nearpod

Enable learners to join a class

As illustrated above, learners can join a class by entering the code. This code can be displayed on the board or shared via email, Facebook, Twitter or Google+. The latter options would suit homework or flipped learning activities. When the learners have joined the class, the teacher is able to display both the website and what the learners see on their tablets.

Image 16.2 Sharing is caring: how to join a Nearpod class

Add slides

You can add a PDF, audio, PowerPoint, GIF, video or any other file. Nearpod also stores three-dimensional images and these are arranged in categories, for example, 'the human body', 'ancient times' or 'the environment'.

For even more variety to your content, there are images and presentations on Sway, Office 365's interactive storytelling app.

'Add an activity'

You can enrich your lessons with an open-ended question, a poll or a quiz or you could ask your learners to draw their answers or ideas. You can also build memory tests by searching for images on

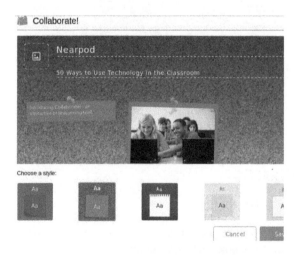

Image 16.3 Compare this brainstorming tool to Padlet

Bing, then simply dragging those images into a square. If you like Padlet's collaborative functionality, you could select 'collaborate!' and use a virtual corkboard to brainstorm ideas for new topics, prior knowledge or revision.

Nearpod for assessment

One of Nearpod's strongest selling points is real-time feedback. Below is a selection of ways to assess using Nearpod.

My library

You can add your own presentations or ones that you have downloaded to 'my library'.

Live session

The 'live session' option makes the lesson available for every student who has successfully entered the code. When conducting a quiz, for example, the teacher's screen will be populated with the learners' scores for each question. It will also display a graph of the percentage of students who answered correctly, which you might want to hide from the class.

Reports

The 'reports' function provides data on student participation rate and correct answer ratios. The former function would be particularly useful for homework of flipped learning activities, though you may want to think about how you would respond to homework excuses.

Draw it

This is an efficient way for the teacher to generate evidence of assessed work. For example, if the question is a mathematical problem and the answer is an equation, learners can hand-write the answer. The teacher can then grade this – maybe while the class are busy with another activity – and the results will be revealed in the usual ways (for example, student by student, percentage correct).

Nearpod for learning

Teachers who want to use Nearpod (or similar) would be advised to consider how they may need to rearrange their classroom. For example, if the teacher arranges the room in a crescent shape, and sits in the centre of the crescent, she or he will be in a better position to offer support and manage behaviour. The reasons for this are that learners will be working extensively on mobile devices and the teacher will be a guide on the side, not a *sage on the stage* (Sams and Bergmann, 2012). It will be crucial to ensure that this is not a cosmetic intervention; rearranging a learning space cannot be on a whim.

Nearpod may offer to change the learning environment but it could, if misused, replicate existing poor-performing pedagogies. One example of this would be retaining the practice of transmitting knowledge and teacher-directed tasks (Hattie, 2008, p245). An antidote to this can be reverse-engineering lessons, so that they begin with the desired outcomes and build a stronger sense of self-regulation (Hattie, 2008).

Another way in which we must be careful with how we assess using Nearpod is that we may fall victim to the tyranny of the right answer and a preponderance of low-order thinking. This is why applying an appropriate 'wait time' (Rowe, 1986) is so important as it helps learners develop meta-cognition and address their own misconceptions (Fisher and Frey, 2014).

Links to the Teachers' Standards

S1: Stretch and challenge

Teachers will welcome the ability to pose spontaneous high-order questions while the lessons are in progress. Also, the 'draw it' function is so quick that it will be easy to ask learners to improve on their previous work.

S2: Promote good progress and outcomes by pupils

The varied features can be efficient ways to build on prior knowledge, for example, polls, brain-storming, missing-word activities and quizzes.

S3: Demonstrate good subject and curriculum knowledge

The immersive features, like GIFs, 360-degree video and three-dimensional images, are likely to foster interest and indulge the teacher's passions.

S4: Plan and teach well-structured lessons

The aforementioned array of activities must not be at the expense of offline activity. Incorporating the analogue skills necessary for passing exams can be an opportunity to improve the pace of your lessons.

S5: Adapt to the strengths and needs of all pupils

The challenge is to use a differentiation checklist close to you when creating activities or questions.

S6: Make accurate and productive use of assessment

As a formative assessment tool, Nearpod is one of the best. Teachers can generate instant records of progress and understanding, to set targets and plan in advance.

S7: Manage behaviour effectively to ensure a good and safe environment

The relative autonomy and potential for distraction on Nearpod make it especially important to communicate clear expectations.

References

Fisher, D, Frey, N (2014) *Checking for Understanding*. Alexandria, VA: ASCD.

Hattie, J (2008) *Visible Learning: A Synthesis of Over 800 Meta-Analyses Relating to Achievement*. London: Routledge.

Rowe, M (1986) Wait time: slowing down may be a way of speeding up! *Journal of Teacher Education*, 37(1): 43–50. Available online at: http://jte.sagepub.com/cgi/content/abstract/37/1/43 [accessed 15 September 2017].

Sams, A, Bergmann, J (2012) *Flip Your Classroom: Reach Every Student in Every Class Every Day*. Washington: International Society for Technology in Education/ISTE.

17
Turnitin

What is Turnitin?

Turnitin is known widely as a plagiarism detection tool. Its originality check feature compares an assignment submitted via Turnitin to millions of papers. This helps maintain integrity and detect dishonesty.

This chapter, though, is not concerned with academic malpractice, however serious this issue may be. There is a growing school of thought that Turnitin can be used as a formative tool, to help writing skills. Here, we will examine how Turnitin can be a supportive, creative tool to help develop and improve learners' writing skills, not just to detect plagiarism.

Turnitin has long been associated solely with higher education. This chapter will focus on the secondary and further education (FE) sectors. The latest thinking emphasises that instances of plagiarism could be avoided if we use Turnitin as a formative tool. Instead of detecting, then punishing, plagiarism, teachers could equip students with an answer to the question: What does plagiarism *not* look like?

What can Turnitin do for teachers and learners?

For teachers

Teachers may be interested in re-evaluating the function of Turnitin. If they saw it as an operational system designed to achieve consistency and enhance academic writing, it could open up some opportunities to work more collaboratively and transparently with the learners. The drive is increasingly towards encouraging learners to cite appropriately and, in doing so, improving academic writing. Below is a breakdown of how they intend to do this.

Feedback

Teachers can mark digitally on PC or tablet and offer rich and meaningful feedback. Turnitin can also be used to help students self-check academic writing.

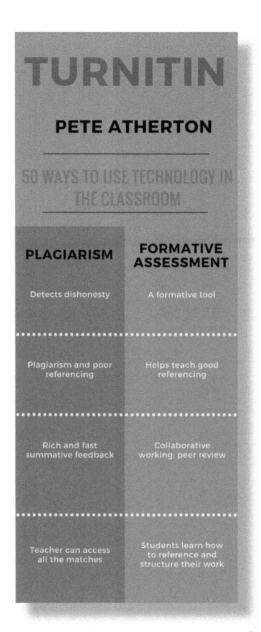

TURNITIN

PETE ATHERTON

50 WAYS TO USE TECHNOLOGY IN THE CLASSROOM

PLAGIARISM	FORMATIVE ASSESSMENT
Detects dishonesty	A formative tool
Plagiarism and poor referencing	Helps teach good referencing
Rich and fast summative feedback	Collaborative working: peer review
Teacher can access all the matches	Students learn how to reference and structure their work

Image 17.1 Infographic: benefits of Turnitin

Audio feedback

Audio feedback is becoming increasingly popular. Turnitin offers this facility and you may want to try it with your students.

The originality check checks learners' work against millions of papers. The report can be seen on the document viewer. Teachers can click on source to see source and comparison. When the teacher or instructor clicks the match button, all the matches can be seen.

For learners

Peer mark

Students' work can be peer-reviewed. This can help build engagement with their peers. Also, the following features are there as a guide to appropriate writing:

- pre-writing;

- redrafting;

- self-check tool.

Peer review

Again this process may be borrowed from universities, but it does have significant potential in secondary school and FE. Peer feedback is, of course, anonymous. After the first phase of peer feedback, students are expected to follow the academic guidelines and make changes. In-depth guidelines for the process of peer reviewing can be found here: **https://guides.turnitin.com/01_Manuals_and_Guides/Student_Guides/Turnitin_Classic/19_PeerMark**.

Image 17.2 Peer review at secondary level too

How to use Turnitin

Students can be protected from plagiarism through Turnitin but building a powerful assessment strategy requires a great deal of infrastructure (Bostock and Taylor, 2014). The following tips should make the process more palatable and help identify how that infrastructure would need to be built.

Dropbox

You may want to ask all departments to liaise with the exams department so that the settings for the dropbox are consistent. The configuration for the dropbox should be standardised to avoid confusion or inconsistencies.

Rubrics

You can make your own rubric or adapt an existing one. There are several examples of ready-to-import rubrics here: **http://www.turnitinuk.com/en_gb/resources/teaching-tools**.

Emergency protocols

If the system goes down they have an automatic 2-week extension. You will need a wide-scale contingency plan for technical problems.

Turnitin for learning

One of the most emotionally precarious aspects of learner feedback can be the perception of an asymmetrical power relationship (McCormack, 2016). Turnitin can mitigate the emotional impact of feedback in a number of ways and these are discussed below.

Ratings for top student sources

Could empowering students to understand why certain sources have more credibility than others help rebalance that power relationship (McCormack, 2016)?

Turnitin have published a guide to the most (and least) useful websites for secondary and higher education. They have formulated the Source Educational Evaluation Rubric (SEER) (Turnitin.com, 2017) to score a selection of websites on their authority, educational value, intent, originality, quality and number of matches. For example, learners will be advised that the *New York Times* is scored as 4 out of 4 for authority because it is widely referenced by others. At the other end of the spectrum, 123Helpme.com gains only 0.5, as much of the information is neither researched nor cited. A full report can be found here: **file:///Users/peteath/Downloads/Turnitin_SEER_Rubric%20(1).pdf.**

Despite its sophistication in detecting plagiarism, it could be argued that Turnitin is merely a text-matching tool; hence, the detection of plagiarism requires professional judgement (Jones, 2008). Its greatest strength as it enters its next phase is in improving learners' confidence and competence (O'Hara et al., 2007).

Links to the Teachers' Standards

S1: Set high expectations which inspire, motivate and challenge pupils

Turnitin can be an effective way to introduce and reinforce appropriate conduct for the creation and submission of work.

S2: Promote good progress and outcomes by pupils

Turnitin encourages learners to redraft their work based on rich feedback.

(Continued)

(Continued)

S5: Adapt to the strengths and needs of all pupils

Feedback can be tailored to the strengths and needs of the learners. For example, some may prefer audio feedback.

S6: Make accurate and productive use of assessment

In terms of formative assessment, Turnitin's advantages include fast, rich feedback, peer review and the ability to be assessed on referencing skills before final submission.

S8: Fulfil wider professional responsibilities

Exam boards welcome the rigour and transparency of Turnitin.

References

Bostock, J, Taylor, L (2014) *Using Turnitin as a Formative Assessment Tool to Support Academic Writing.* SOLSTICE/CLT Conference, 21 June 2017, Edge Hill University.

Jones, KO (2008) Practical issues for academics using the Turnitin plagiarism detection software. Paper presented at the International Conference on Computer Systems and Technology.

McCormack, M (2016) Feedback without tears: student responses to feedback. LJMU Teaching and Learning Conference 2016. Liverpool: Higher Education Academy/LJMU Curriculum Enhancement Fund.

O'Hara, M, Carter, C, Manassee, G (2007) *Getting It Write: A Multidisciplinary Approach to Student Academic Support – A JISCPAS Case Study.* Available online at: http://www.plagiarismadvice.org/resources/engaging-students/item/ohara-casestudy [accessed 3 October 2017].

Turnitin.com (2017) *Turnitin: Ratings for Top Student Sources.* Available online at: http://www.turnitin.com/assets/en_us/media/seer/se/academic.php#.WVqOrNPytxg [accessed 3 July 2017].

Social media

18
Facebook

What is Facebook, in the context of teaching and learning?

Just about everyone who is reading this book will know that Facebook is an online social network. In terms of its educational value, it has its uses but, as with every social media platform, there will need to be rigorous contracting and close monitoring of activity, to minimise the chance of cyber-bullying or posting of inappropriate content. These issues will be touched upon in this chapter.

Before we focus on the potential to use Facebook in or outside a classroom, it is worth noting that it already has functions that can be seen elsewhere, for instance, polling apps, direct messaging, the ability to post links and multimedia content. It is also emphasising one basic piece of advice – please do not follow students, under any circumstances. If you don't think this is obvious, please ask your colleagues and they will tell you why.

What can Facebook do for teachers and learners?

For teachers

Storing resources

Facebook can be a convenient way for teachers to store large files in a location that will be discoverable for the learners. This can remove the risk of slowing down your institution's network and can reduce the chance of learners claiming that they are unaware of the location of certain content.

Paper status updates

The fact that this chapter is about using Facebook in the classroom does not necessarily mean that all activity has to be online. Facebook updates can be simulated by using one of many online templates (search for 'Facebook status update template'). An example of how learners could use this is by replying to a speech by a character in a play by way of a hand-written status update on Facebook. Doing this minimises the risk of de-skilling learners' traditional literacies.

Image 18.1 Infographic: benefits of using Facebook

For learners

Teaching social media skills

Social media responsibility, literacies and skills can be taught through Facebook. Learners could be given their assignments but directed to an activity beforehand, in which they have to respond to a variety of scenarios. Examples of these could be:

- how to be legal;

- how to create a profile that is appropriate;

- how to be safe and responsible;

- how to avoid litigation;

- how to avoid breaking the school rules;

- how to separate the personal from the professional.

Treasure hunts

If teachers create a Facebook group for their class or subject, they could post regular updates, sometimes unexpectedly. These updates could be questions, resources, quizzes, polls, teasers based on images or diagrams, and so on. Teachers would need to comply with the school's policy on social media communication, especially if the updates were outside hours.

Creative writing

Posting Facebook updates as a character from literature, history, business, even science could work well as long as there has been considerable research from the learners and planning from the teacher.

Facebook for assessment

Facebook Live

Before examining some of the ways that Facebook can be used to assess students' work, it may be useful to provide an example of using Facebook Live to stream specific guidance regarding assignments. See **http://socialmediaexplorer.com/content-sections/tools-and-tips/use-facebook-live-drive-traffic-subscribers-website/**.

Assessing through closed Facebook groups

Closed Facebook groups can be powerful ways to show evidence of formative assessment. Examples of this can be videoing practical demonstrations in small groups and asking the learners to peer assess. The teacher could then provide some formative feedback, before repeating the process with an improved piece of work. Examples of relevant pieces of work could be:

- scientific experiments;

- monologues;

- screen recordings of content from learners' mobile phones – apps like iRec enable this;

- drama or dance performances;

- specific teaching points in PE or sport;

- business or film pitches.

Facebook for learning

Facebook, along with other technology giants like Microsoft, Google and Apple, are keen to tap into the growing edtech market. From 2016, one of the focuses of Facebook's attention was the learning management system (LMS) market (Boorstin, 2017). Facebook built the software for personal learning plans for Summit schools in the USA (Cox, 2015). These LMSs are built to monitor pupils' cognitive skills and focus areas in specific subjects. One of the by-products of this policy may be that Facebook can be perceived as ethical and contributing to a better society. This could be a judicious tactic in light of the negative publicity that major corporations sometimes attract.

Links to the Teachers' Standards

S1: Set high expectations which inspire, motivate and challenge pupils

Facebook's company info page (Cox, 2015) stipulates that they promote a culture of creative problem solving. This could be worth engaging with in a way that can foster these skills in the learners to help stretch and challenge.

S2: Promote good progress and outcomes by pupils

Being aware of how pupils learn can mean asking them how they would like to learn through Facebook.

S3: Demonstrate good subject and curriculum knowledge

The idea of the teacher posting regular teasers and background reading/viewing shows both your students and colleagues that you have a keen and active subject knowledge.

S4: Plan and teach well-structured lessons

Facebook activities can add a welcome variety to lessons. A closed Facebook group can inject currency and inclusivity.

S5: Adapt to the strengths and needs of all pupils

There are many ways for learners to research, demonstrate their learning and express themselves through Facebook.

S6: Make accurate and productive use of assessment

As with other social platforms, closed Facebook groups can give evidence of formative feedback.

S7: Manage behaviour effectively to ensure a good and safe environment

Facebook can be an effective way to teach about appropriate conduct, legality and ethics.

S8: Fulfil wider professional responsibilities

Your use of Facebook could lead the way in how your school uses technology enhanced learning.

References

Boorstin, J (2017) *A $16 Billion Education Tech Market That Microsoft, Facebook and Google Are Studying*. CNBC. Available online at: http://www.cnbc.com/2017/03/28/microsoft-google-and-facebook-see-billions-in-future-of-education.html [accessed 5 June 2017].

Cox, C. (2015) *Introducing Facebook and Summit's K-12 Education Project | Facebook Newsroom*. Newsroom.fb.com. Available online at: https://newsroom.fb.com/news/2015/09/introducing-facebook-and-summits-k-12-education-project/ [accessed 5 June 2017].

19
Twitter

Image 19.1 My own Twitter profile @Petestarryid

What is Twitter?

Twitter may have spent its early years as a marginal platform for podcasters but it is now a global microblogging phenomenon. The extent of Twitter's prominence as a platform extends to tweets regularly being part of public discourse. For example, Donald Trump's rise to power has been partly attributed to his harnessing of Twitter to influence conversations in bars and workplaces and in the mainstream media.

While Trump's improbable ascent may divide opinion, it has been rich in social media content that demands to be deconstructed. In that respect, Trump's Twitter is like any other high-profile feed: it invites further investigation, it is successful in communicating within tight parameters and it manages to motivate students to find alternative viewpoints.

Image 19.2 Infographic: benefits of using Twitter for education

What can Twitter do for teachers and learners?

For teachers

Twitter's potential uses in the classroom are manifold. As teachers become more savvy with their digital literacies, their learners can expect to embed social media into their learning. Before considering how, it may be sensible to think about what *not* to do.

How not to use Twitter as a teacher

- Follow students
- Try and be funny or cool - everything you post can be screen saved, shared and decontextualised
- No images or poorly lit, distant images with little thought for composition
- No hashtags
- Too many hashtags
- No tagging (you do this by adding @ to a Twitter handle)
- Post a few times, then not at all
- No info on the profile
- Reply to direct messages (DMs)

The Twitter for learning section goes into more depth about how to ensure that Twitter communication matches the platform. Before you (re)launch your school Twitter, use the search bar to look for teachers who have thousands of followers and whose tweets gain traction. Join a few relevant Twitter lists by googling 'Twitter lists (my subject)'. In terms of approaching your Twitter with the correct mindset, try to position yourself as an expert in your subject, but remember that expertise can often be through your curation of other people's content.

As with any social platform, using Twitter carries risks. You may wish to send a letter to all parents before you begin any Twitter project. Despite these warnings, the best way to do it is to jump right in. You can have a healthy and active Twitter feed if you set aside 20 minutes in the morning and 20 minutes in the early evening.

For learners

Here is a short summary of ways that learners could benefit from Twitter.

- Using Twitter can help learners explore literary characters, famous innovators or scientists by tweeting as them.

- This platform can teach people about the conventions of certain types of tweet. Hashtags, for example, can be used to categorise but also in creative ways that can defy grammatical rules.

- Twitter can frame debates about personal and social educational/personal development and ethics.

- Twitter lists help learners find relevant content for their subject.

- A student could experience on Twitter the thrill of having a reply, like or retweet from a distinguished authority in your subject.

How to use Twitter for educational purposes

The following are ways in which Twitter can be used to increase learners' engagement in your subject.

Hashtags (#)

As with anything in the world of social media, hashtags have evolved considerably. They provide identity tags for topics and issues, to make it easier for users to search for and follow these.

Twitter lists

Ask the group to subscribe to 'lists' that relate to your subject.

Communication

Use a recognisable hashtag to communicate resources and important information about assignments to the learners. In some cases, an entire formative assignments could be submitted through Twitter. Twitter polls can garner clear, quick and easy feedback on learners' feelings towards issues and topics being studied.

Remember: like any kind of communication with learners, teachers may want to note that every tweet is transparent and open to (mis)interpretation. Please take your own advice and choose your words carefully; be cautious but try not to be paranoid or put off using Twitter altogether.

Research skills

Use 'social listening' tools to listen in on real-time conversations on a given topic.

If you want to find out what people are saying about, say, Brexit in the Birmingham area, simply follow these steps:

1. Enter 'Brexit' in the search box.

2. Click on 'More' in the 'Advanced search'.

3. Narrow the search results further, for example, relating to a specific hashtag. Search results can even be categorised by their sentiment, for example, 'positive', 'negative' and 'question'.

Another way of geolocating searches is by using tools like Trendsmap and Tweepsmap. Sites like these go a little deeper than native Twitter by showing a map of trending tweets by location. Both, however, require users to sign up.

Tweet walls

Encourage and capture questions: a section of your lesson could be used to ask learners to post questions on a tweet wall (these are easy to set up on Tweetwall.com).

Would you like your Twitter feed to be the best in the school?

Twitter for learning

The reality for many teachers is that they will use Twitter sparingly and usually for personal development, which is sometimes viewed as superior to paid courses (Krutka and Cunningham, 2016). Conversely, training events and conferences can be essential ways to network with existing or potential collaborators and educators with similar interests. It can also discover new teaching materials, research in your field or policies (Cunningham, 2017).

Links to the Teachers' Standards

S1: Set high expectations which inspire, motivate and challenge pupils

Communicating knowledge in 140 characters (280 from November 2017) and through a specific channel helps develop deep learning.

S2: Promote good progress and outcomes by pupils

If learners are given the kudos of being the ones to discover and share good quality updates on their subjects, this could help them take a responsible and conscientious attitude to their studies.

S3: Demonstrate good subject and curriculum knowledge

Teachers can position themselves as experts in their subject on Twitter, but make sure you offer something of value.

S4: Plan and teach well-structured lessons

Twitter activities can be so varied and diverse that they can be a regular feature of learning both inside and outside the classroom.

S5: Adapt to the strengths and needs of all pupils

In-class activities and active engagement can help teaching create a truly differentiated classroom.

S6: Make accurate and productive use of assessment

Use tools to help assess through Twitter (e.g. Tweetcred, which assesses the credibility of sources).

S7: Manage behaviour effectively to ensure a good and safe environment

Without carefully considering rules and making expectations clear, your Twitter adventure would be ill advised.

S8: Fulfil wider professional responsibilities

Consider using Twitter for personal, health and social education. Also, Twitter can be very useful for exploring equality and diversity issues.

References

Cunningham, M (2017) Teachers on Twitter: is it CPD? *SecEd*. Available online at: http://www.sec-ed.co.uk/best-practice/teachers-on-twitter-is-it-cpd/ [accessed 28 September 2017].

Krutka, D, Carpenter, J (2016) Participatory learning through social media: how and why social studies educators use Twitter. *Contemporary Issues in Technology and Teacher Education*, 16(1). Available online at: http://www.citejournal.org/volume-16/issue-1-16/social-studies/participatory-learning-through-social-media-how-and-why-social-studies-educators-use-twitter [accessed 20 October 2017].

20
Snapchat

What is Snapchat?

Snapchat is diversifying beyond its unique value proposition of a photo-messaging app that deletes photos a short time after they are taken. From the outset, this was the main difference between Snapchat and Instagram. The platform's popularity grew quickly from its launch in 2011. Snapchat's user base grew to 100 million per day in March 2017 (Mediakix, 2016). It was the introduction of Snapchat Stories in 2013 that began to offer features that may be of interest in terms of pedagogy.

What can Snapchat do for teachers and learners?

For teachers

Whether you are a digital immigrant, a digital native or a settler (Ingle and Duckworth, 2013), it is clear that Snapchat's functionality is in a state of rapid change. This may be enticing for those voracious users whose peers can inform them about new features, but the challenge for many will be remaining current.

Snapchat Stories

Improving literacy can be encouraged by asking individuals or pairs to create snaps through taking amusing or memorable photographs, then adding visually appealing text alongside the image. Learners could be coached on how to take a screenshot of the new image and then sharing it, perhaps on the same Padlet wall.

For learners
Sending Snaps to each other

You may want to think very carefully about peer-to-peer communication on Snapchat for educational purposes. You would need to consult senior managers at your institution and take advice about IT policy and safeguarding.

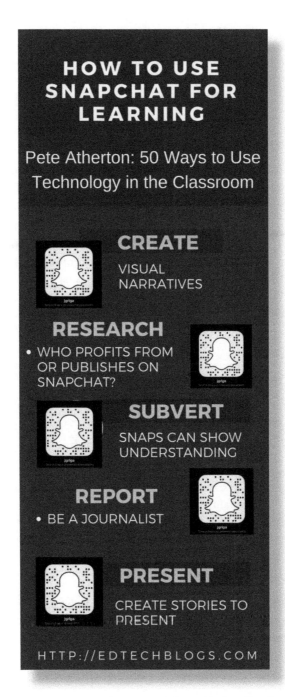

Image 20.1 Infographic: benefits of using Snapchat for learning

It could be preferable to capitalise on the ways in which Snapchat Stories can help users create disruptive, subversive and highly creative narratives.

Snapchat Stories

Learners could make a series of very short films to summarise what they have learned in your lessons. They could also become journalists, producing parodies or amusing reports related to their learning. They could also have fun by face swapping with their friends to create a journalistic persona.

How to use Snapchat

At its most basic level, users can create 'snaps' by taking photos by tapping the camera icon at the foot of the screen or record videos by holding down the same button. They can then edit those 'snaps' by adding text and emojis and by drawing. Selecting 'Memories' enables you to upload and edit your previous snaps and photographs and videos from your camera roll.

Whichever way learners are using Snapchat, they will have access to privileged information about how to use it. The platform is becoming more immersive by introducing new features on a regular basis, for example, icons, filters and lenses. For example, snaps can be augmented by drawing shapes using emojis or looping videos. Using an element of the functionality of Photoshop parts of an image can be erased. Moreover, the multitude of related apps provide a growing supply of customisation options.

Snapchat for assessment

Snapchat may not be the first social media platform that teachers call to mind when considering how to assess their learners but it is worth investigating.

Research

Ask learners to use Snapchat to research Snapchat accounts that are relevant to their subject. They could then be assessed on the quality of their presentation or annotated catalogue of sources. For example, *National Geographic* is one of many magazines who use the Discover platform to reach Snapchat users with accessible, educational content. The same can be said of @Generalelectric.

Making snaps as mini-presentations

The appeal of this is that these short videos can be saved to learners' own devices, then shared via the virtual learning environment or a third-party application like Padlet. The implications for developing subject knowledge, literacy and numeracy in this way are considerable. Students could even explore technical, scientific or IT aspects of Snapchat, for example, how Snapchat lenses work.

Snapchat for learning

Offline content

As with many social media platforms, the content can be parodied or pastiched offline.

Creativity

Learners can add a snap by taking a picture of their work, their computer, an object, another learner and so on. They can then add text, emojis and drawings to clarify, reinforce, change or subvert the meaning.

Employability

Social media can offer an enticing glimpse into the world of work. Asking learners to deconstruct and analyse how celebrated Snapchatters work and make money could help raise learners' aspirations and manage their expectations. Examples of potential role models are @SophiaAmoruso and @Evachen from the world of fashion entrepreneurship. To plug into this, learners could be asked to apply for a specific job through making a Snapchat story, as a growing number of companies are requesting from their applicants (Najjar, 2016).

Snapchat is worth watching very closely in terms of its ability to chronicle the progression from the expected behaviours of digital natives (Prensky, 2012; Ingle and Duckworth, 2013) to the notion of *creative problem solving* (Jenkins, 2009) for millennials through emerging technologies.

Links to the Teachers' Standards

S1: Set high expectations which inspire, motivate and challenge pupils

Snapchat's technical versatility as a platform can create many opportunities for learners to break through the glass ceiling of achievement.

S2: Promote good progress and outcomes by pupils

Snapchat can provide a narrative of how learners have built on prior knowledge.

S5: Adapt to the strengths and needs of all pupils

If you make the success criteria differentiated, you can use Snapchat to prove that the tasks, questioning and outcome have been successfully differentiated.

S6: Make accurate and productive use of assessment

Snapchat Stories can show that learners have acted on feedback. Peers can annotate work by adding text to snaps. Learners can document how they have acted on feedback about their snaps by adding text and emojis.

References

Ingle, S, Duckworth, V (2013) *Enhancing Learning Through Technology in Lifelong Learning*. Maidenhead: McGraw-Hill.

Jenkins, H (2009) *Confronting the Challenges of Participatory Culture: Media Education for the 21st Century (The John D. and Catherine T. MacArthur Foundation Reports on Digital Media and Learning)*. Cambridge, MA: MIT Press.

Mediakix (2016) *The Snapchat Statistics Every Marketer Needs to Know*. Available online at: http://mediakix.com/2016/01/snapchat-statistics-2016-marketers-need-to-know/#gs.gCD7sJ0 [accessed 28 September 2017].

Najjar, C (2016) *9 Snapchat Accounts to Follow to Make You Smarter, Craftier, and Richer*. Teen Vogue. Available online at: http://www.teenvogue.com/story/9-snapchat-accounts-make-you-smarter [accessed 17 May 2017].

Prensky, M (2012) *From Digital Natives to Digital Wisdom*. London: SAGE Publications.

21

Instagram

What is Instagram?

Instagram began as a photo-sharing platform. Now owned by Facebook, its fast-evolving functionality now incorporates live video. To illustrate the pace of change in the world of social media, it took radio 38 years to gain an audience of 50 million people; television reached the same number in just 13 years; Instagram took just 1½ years to acquire 50 million users (Vaynerchuk, 2013).

What can Instagram do for teachers and learners?

For teachers

On Instagram, hashtags are a crucial way to categorise content and make your own posts more visible and searchable. Each post can use a maximum of 30 hashtags. Apps like Hashme and Tagboard can reveal the most popular hashtags used in certain categories. Subsequently, an Instagram post about edtech is more likely to go viral if you also add hashtags sourced through Hashme or Tagboard. At the time of writing, these included #teacherproblems, #teacherlife and #education – and many more.

Searching using the hashtag #TeachersFollowTeachers or #TeachersOfInstagram allows you to discover resources that may refresh your teaching. These can be broad, for example, #Googleedu #STEM of #science. They can also be specific or niche: geology teachers may want to search using the hashtag #Geologyrocks or #Geologyporn to discover posts that can provide stimulus material that is native to their learners' internet activity.

For learners

As of June 2017, the social media preferences of millennials (or those born around 2000) showed a continuing dedication to Facebook and Instagram but not Twitter. Around 30% preferred Facebook, 20% Instagram but only about 5% preferred Twitter (Chen, 2017). It may be useful for teachers to be armed with empirical data for occasions when learners (justifiably) claim ownership of all social media and hence pass judgement on specific platforms. This data is changing as quickly as the fickle habits of millennials, so try to keep abreast of new developments.

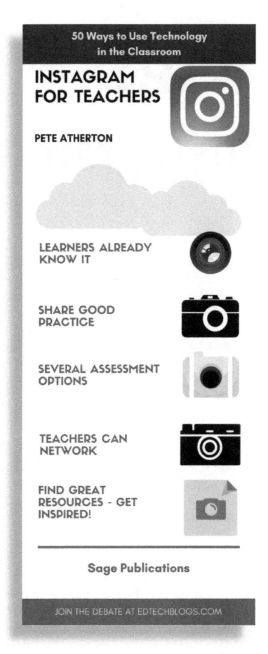

Image 21.1 Infographic: benefits of using Instagram

How to use Instagram

Instagram is not alone in being highly user-friendly but it may still intimidate some. Here is a ten-step programme to get you started.

1. Download the Instagram app to your smartphone (via the App Store or Google Play).

2. Make an account.

3. Create a profile, including a photo.

4. Use the search icon at the bottom to seek out relevant posts.

5. Double tap to like a post.

6. Tap the speech bubble icon to comment.

Now make a post:

7. Tap the + icon to add a photo.

8. Upload a good quality (well-lit, meaningful) image or video from your photo library.

9. Add short but engaging text – try to make it enhance the image like a slogan.

10. Add up to 30 relevant hashtags (#), maybe sourced through Tagboard or Hashme.

You may want to ask for help from someone who is already confident on Instagram. If you still balk at the idea of posting your own images, try the Repost app, which allows you to repost other people's content on your own page.

Instagram for assessment

One of the most popular way for students to create assessed work through Instagram is by using it as a way of curating other people's creativity. When they do post their own photos, videos, text, emojis and hashtags, each could have separate success criteria. For example, the photo could be of learners working in pairs to create a mind map, diagram, experiment, performance, equation and so on. The emoji could be a way for learners to express how they feel about the work. They may want to express the mood of their performance piece or the results of their experiment. The hashtags will help place the work in categories and some could be used as a witty, expressive coda at the end of a post (Vaynerchuk, 2013).

Since Instagram embraced video and live streaming, the platform presented new ways for learners to show their understanding. If learners post using given hashtags and tag the teacher's account by adding @ to their username, they can then peer assess by commenting on posts. Once the peer assessment has been completed, the teacher can offer his own feedback. The learners can then use an analysis of the discussion to determine their next course of action, which can be assessed by the teacher in their own way.

Instagram for learning

This form of assessment is an example of a connectivist classroom, where learning is not imposed but facilitated, negotiated and reviewed collaboratively through technology (Siemens, 2005). In true connectivist style, some of the initial peer assessment could even be outsourced to relevant users, who could be tagged and asked for feedback.

Using Instagram is a one of many ways of employing edtech in a way that follows Puentedura's (2014, cited in Walsh, 2015) SAMR model (substitution, augmentation, modification and redefinition). This model was created to help educators use technology in more effective ways. In terms of using Instagram for learning, the substitution could be learners photographing what is on the whiteboard, instead of writing it down. The augmentation could be attained by the use of hashtags to organise learners' own photos and curate others. Modification would involve posting comments on each other's work, then tagging their peers and selected social media influencers. Finally, redefinition could require learners to post a video – live or otherwise – to demonstrate, summarise or synthesise their knowledge.

Links to the Teachers' Standards

S1: Set high expectations which inspire, motivate and challenge pupils

If learners 'go native' (i.e. use platforms that they are familiar with), the technology does not get in the way of progress. It also frees them up to take risks and experiment.

S2: Promote good progress and outcomes by pupils

The challenge here will be turning a familiar platform into a platform for learning. In that respect, mastery goals need to be made clear.

S3: Demonstrate good subject and curriculum knowledge

Teachers can use hashtags to find inspiration and resources and share good practice.

S4: Plan and teach well-structured lessons

Instagram could help the structure of lessons as part of a flipped classroom.

S5: Adapt to the strengths and needs of all pupils

Instagram helps embrace various learning styles and multimodal literacies.

S6: Make accurate and productive use of assessment

If the success criteria are clear and negotiated, Instagram could be a rewarding way to facilitate and showcase assessed work.

S7: Manage behaviour effectively to ensure a good and safe environment

Please refer to the terms of use and departmental/school-wide social media policy before embarking on your journey.

References

Chen, J (2017) Instagram vs. Snapchat: which is best for your business? *Sproutsocial*. Available online at: https://sproutsocial.com/insights/instagram-vs-snapchat/ [accessed 28 September 2017].

Siemens, G (2005) *Connectivism: A Learning Theory for the Digital Age*. Available online at: http://www.itdl.org/journal/jan_05/article01.htm [accessed 20 July 2016].

Vaynerchuk, G (2013) *Jab, Jab, Jab, Right Hook*. New York, NY: HarperBusiness.

Walsh, K (2015) *8 Examples of Transforming Lessons Through the SAMR Cycle*. Available online at: http://www.emergingedtech.com/2015/04/examples-of-transforming-lessons-through-samr/ [accessed 11 August 2017].

22
Tumblr

What is Tumblr?

Tumblr is a blogging platform that was bought by Yahoo for $1.1bn in 2013. Like Pinterest, it can be an exhibition space for the creative industries but it also has a reputation for activism (Hughes, 2017). For example, Tumblr have spearheaded their own campaigns, such as their opposition to Society for Online Piracy (SOPA).

What can Tumblr do for teachers and learners?

For teachers

Before you begin, you could ask some parents and your head teacher about how they would deal with the possibility of a child being caught at home watching adult content on Tumblr, then blaming it on you. Inappropriate content, of course, is not exclusive to Tumblr and your school should also have a clear policy on internet use outside the classroom.

Some other preliminary work could be to view what school children are already producing on Tumblr.

You may also wish to capitalise on Tumblr's reputation for activism and ask your students to use it to run a campaign. Here are some suggestions for subject-specific campaigns:

- Lab Force: change the world with science;
- World of Maths: the maths awareness campaign;
- Word Up!: the campaign for a bigger vocabulary;
- Our Story: solving today's issues with history.

For learners

You will need to balance your learners' desire for autonomy and creativity with their reliance on and need for scaffolding. With that in mind, it would probably be best if you began by printing out, displaying and deconstructing some Tumblr posts. How could this tie in with the learning objectives in your subject?

Image 22.1 Infographic: benefits of using Tumblr

How to use Tumblr

The interface below is worth displaying as a starting point before your learners become immersed in their own phonescapes. This is, in essence, the anatomy of a Tumblr post.

Image 22.2

GIFs

GIF is an acronym for graphics interchange format. In 2012, it was the word of the year in the *Oxford English Dictionary*. GIFs may have lost much of their novelty value but are, like emojis, still a notable form of non-verbal communication to express emotion or virtual affinity.

Tumblr for assessment

Now that you know the conventions and structure of a Tumblr post, you could consider asking the learners to sketch a Tumblr post on paper. This would clearly double as a literacy task, where support and feedback would be given on spelling, punctuation and grammar.

Textual analysis

An obvious way to start to analyse Tumblr posts is on paper, with colour displays on the whiteboard. Vaynerchuk's (2013) slating of some Tumblr campaigns and positive discussion of others reveal a great deal about the importance of social media literacy. You could, perhaps, ask the learners to use these critiques to draw up a style guide for posting on Tumblr.

Tumblr versus another social media platform

Try to ask the learners to compose a comparative analysis of the conventions of communication on Tumblr, Facebook, Snapchat or Instagram. Learners will, of course, display fierce loyalties towards what they consider to be the most in vogue social media platform. They may feel that Tumblr is not for them, but the facts suggest otherwise: in late 2016, Tumblr was among the most popular network among 16–24-year-olds, alongside Snapchat and Instagram (McCue, 2016).

Tumblr for learning

Tumblr could be used to teach creativity and develop high-order thinking. If you believe, like De Bono (1967, cited in Dawson, 2005), that creativity is not a talent but a process, a skill to be developed, Tumblr can be part of an ongoing series of homework and flipped learning activities where children can develop confidence in their own creativity.

Learners will be developing and demonstrating the multimodal skills of content curation and dissemination, without the restrictions of gatekeepers (Jenkins, 2009; Duckworth, 2014). These skills are likely to be necessary for the workplace and can enrich and deepen breadth of knowledge and depth of understanding (Duckworth, 2014).

Links to the Teachers' Standards

S1: Stretch and challenge

The space and creativity encouraged on Tumblr could make the learning more immersive. Also, regular feedback from peers and clear, mutually agreed objectives are likely to raise the bar.

S2: Promote good progress and outcomes by pupils

The Tumblr blog could contain all notes, worksheets, research findings and creativity for a unit of work.

S3: Demonstrate good subject and curriculum knowledge

Part of the Tumblr blogging project would need to be led by useful stimulus materials and further reading that the teacher has found.

S4: Plan and teach well-structured lessons

The blogs would build into something meaningful if they were regularly shared, critiqued and celebrated.

(Continued)

(Continued)

S5: Adapt to the strengths and needs of all pupils

Learner blogs provide varied ways of expressing knowledge and ideas. This is likely to embrace different learning styles and abilities.

S6: Make accurate and productive use of assessment

One of the objectives of the blog could be reflecting specifically on feedback and planning how the learner is going to improve next time.

S7: Manage behaviour effectively to ensure a good and safe environment

Pay close attention to your school policy on online activity and safeguarding. Make your expectations clear. Consider using Tumblr for homework only.

References

Dawson, P (2005) *Creative Writing and the New Humanities*. London: Routledge.

Duckworth, V (2014) *How To Be a Brilliant FE Teacher*. London: Routledge.

Hughes, M (2017) How Tumblr reconciles political activism with business. *The Next Web*. Available online at: https://thenextweb.com/insider/2017/05/19/tumblr-reconciles-political-activism-business [accessed 15 September 2017].

Jenkins, H (2009) *Confronting the Challenges of Participatory Culture: Media Education for the 21st Century (The John D. and Catherine T. MacArthur Foundation Reports on Digital Media and Learning)*. Cambridge, MA: MIT Press.

McCue, T (2016) Snapchat, WhatsApp, and Instagram dominating younger demographic. *Forbes*. Available online at: https://www.forbes.com/sites/tjmccue/2016/09/27/snapchat-whatsapp-and-instagram-dominating-younger-demographic/#331d61a069fc [accessed 15 July 2017].

Vaynerchuk, G (2013) *Jab, Jab, Jab, Right Hook*. New York: HarperCollins.

23
Pinterest

What is Pinterest?

Pinterest is a virtual pinboard, which is divided into themes, for example, 'cooking' or 'tattoos'. Pinterest is a *portmanteau* word, which combines 'pin' and 'interest': its purpose, then, is to allow users to pin content that they find interesting. People can use a pin button on their browser or the app to pin, repin, send or share pins – all without fear of copyright infringement.

Facebook, Twitter and Instagram may have embraced live video wholeheartedly in 2016 but, as of 2017, Pinterest's main source of content is images. In terms of its educational functions and potential, Pinterest is increasingly popular amongst students and educators.

How to use Pinterest for teachers and learners

For teachers

Use the search box to discover potentially useful content. The search results reveal a combination of photographs, infographics, film stills, art work, cartoons, diagrams, posters and worksheets. Many of these could be adapted, critiqued or presented by learners and displayed around a classroom or a virtual learning environment. Learners could also create their own boards, either by class (for example, Year 10 *Macbeth*) or by theme (for example, 'murder in *Macbeth*').

To narrow the search, the tabs at the top divide the results into subheadings, for example, 'Teaching', 'Art' or 'Witches'.

For learners

Creating their own pinboards

For creative subjects like art, film and media studies, this could function as a mood board. As learners collect, categorise and prioritise images, they could justify and present their choices. In doing so, they would be developing their metacognition and literacy skills. The relevance of their selections and justifications could also be assessed against clear criteria.

Image 23.1 Infographic: benefits of using Pinterest

One of the main benefits of this is that the learners do not need to waste time blindly 'researching' without structure or guidance. The themed tabs enable learners to narrow their searches. For example, asking learners to restrict their research to 'Macbeth' and 'quotes' reveals significant potential for collecting relevant content.

How to use Pinterest

As Pinterest is so simple to use, this is best presented as a step-by-step guide, using bullet points.

- Step 1: Make an account by entering your email and creating a password.

- Step 2: You will then be prompted to build your profile.

- Step 3: Follow some relevant boards.

- Step 4: Create a board.

- Step 5: Decide whether your board is secret or public.

- Step 6: Start searching for topics, boards and people.

- Step 7: Start saving pins to your board.

- Step 8: Practise exporting pins to Twitter and Facebook.

- Step 9: Embed a pin and copy and paste the code on to the virtual learning environment or a website.

- Step 10: Upload an image and link it to a web address (or URL).

Pinterest for assessment

Pinboards

One example of how to assess learners' work through Pinterest could be to ask them to work in pairs to use ten selected pins about mitosis to create a display for the biology website. They could then make a mood board on paper to summarise their findings, then present five points to the class. Students would be rewarded for the clarity and depth of their understanding. They would also receive a grade for spelling, punctuation and grammar.

Mood boards

More frequently, Pinterest can be used to help create mood boards for creative subjects. For example, if art students are assembling ideas for their assignment, Pinterest can stimulate ideas, then help learners communicate their creativity. There are, however, innumerable attractive and very useful resources for all subjects. Try searching for your subject, then view the tabs at the top and the boards and people underneath. You will surely find something that is likely to empower your learners to do the same.

Feedback

If learners work on a board – either alone or in groups – the teacher could leave comments. Once the learners had acted on the advice, their teacher could post further comments.

Pinterest for learning

Could Pinterest help teachers' evidence of formative assessment?

Chapter 1, on formative assessment in the digital age, refers to the new National Curriculum, through which learners must have experienced assessment for learning on discrete units of work before they progress (Fleming, 2012; McIntosh, 2015). This places greater emphasis on a deeper understanding of what students may or may not understand.

This begs the question of whether the aforementioned activities on Pinterest could help develop a deeper understanding of fewer topics (Guskey, 2012, cited in McIntosh, 2015). To make this happen, teachers could consider spending more time communicating the goals of the lesson, perhaps during the preceding one. In that way, the learners could experience much more than merely covering content and completing tasks (Hattie, 2012).

The takeaway from this chapter, then, could be to interrogate the goals that you would wish your learners to attain through Pinterest. A suitable example of just one goal could be, 'By the end of this session, all learners will be encouraged and supported to understand how to make their own pinboard for one of the selected topics'.

Links to the Teachers' Standards

S1: Set high expectations which inspire, motivate and challenge pupils

Because Pinterest is such an efficient way of discovering and saving information, you may want to think carefully about what learners will do with this information.

S2: Promote good progress and outcomes by pupils

Leading on from the point above, will learners be able to communicate the mastery goals to each other (Hattie, 2012)?

S3: Demonstrate good subject and curriculum knowledge

You can use Pinterest to share impressive new resources.

S4: Plan and teach well-structured lessons

Pinterest helps you set varied, fresh and stimulating activities.

S5: Adapt to the strengths and needs of all pupils

Don't forget to differentiate pre-assessment by the design of tasks and questions. Ensure that the success criteria are achievable but offer adequate scaffolding and potential to shine.

S6: Make accurate and productive use of assessment

There are many opportunities for group-based and flipped learning activities but you must ensure that the learners understand the success criteria.

S8: Fulfil wider professional responsibilities

You could make an excellent contribution to school corridors, the virtual learning environment or website through your careful handling of Pinterest.

References

Fleming, P (2012) *Becoming a Secondary School Teacher: How to Make a Success of Your Initial Teacher Training and Induction,* 2nd edition. London: Routledge.

Hattie, J (2012) *Visible Learning: A Synthesis of Over 800 Meta-Analyses Relating to Achievement.* London: Routledge.

McIntosh, K (2015) *Final Report of the Commission on Assessment without Levels.* Available online at: https://www.gov.uk/government/uploads/system/uploads/attachment_data/file/483058/Commission_on_Assessment_Without_Levels_-_report.pdf [accessed 15 August 2016].

24
Learnium

What is Learnium?

Why is Learnium included in the section on social media and edtech? An increasing number of edtech platforms announce themselves as social and suitable for all learning contexts and Learnium is no exception. Learnium hopes that its connected learning will help improve the student experience. At the time of writing it was free for teachers but also offered a paid option for £30 a month, with more advanced admin controls, announcements and analytics.

What can Learnium do for teachers and learners?

For teachers

Teachers commonly use Learnium to:

- communicate with students (often as an alternative to the learning management system (LMS) forum/discussion board, which was deemed unengaging);

- use a social media-style platform safely with students;

- get students to collaborate on documents (for presentation, reports, etc.);

- get students to co-curate (i.e. share relevant resources, files, web bookmarks), sometimes for assessment purposes;

- embed in their existing LMS;

- use it as a neutral ground for projects (with students, peers or researchers) that span across institutions.

You can set social, collaborative projects without having to worry about the potential risks of operating through the major social networks like Facebook and Twitter, which are often blocked in schools.

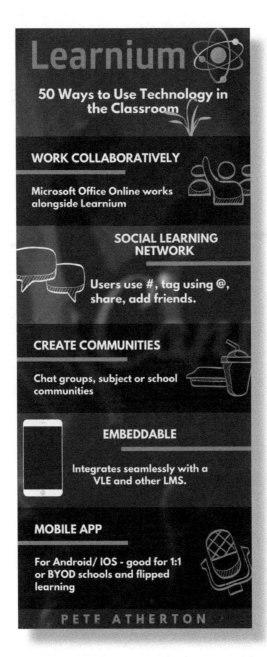

Image 24.1 Infographic: benefits of Learnium

The board feature

This allows teachers to share resources and activities through Microsoft Office Online. As illustrated in Image 24.2, you can make announcements, add new boards, view members and create chat groups.

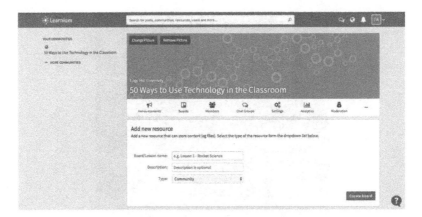

Image 24.2 Board sensible?

Create chat groups

You can encourage your learners to find common ground through these chat groups. You would need to moderate the group and establish rules of acceptable behaviour.

Create communities

Your subject-specific group could be 'Mr/Ms Clarke's History Train' or 'Mr/Ms Graham's Sustainability Society'.

For learners

Students most often use Learnium to:

- communicate with fellow students and teachers;

- give them access to resources shared by the teacher or other students;

- run shadow modules (shadow modules are run by the students themselves to complement teaching that takes place through the core curriculum);

- have contact with their learning space on their mobile device.

There are many opportunities for learners working collaboratively, for example, by working together on essays, presentations, exam answers, research or revision materials. In that sense, Learnium can be a rival to Google Drive in terms of its ease of use.

How to use Learnium

Registering, signing in and creating a network or chat group are as simple as one could hope for in a website.

Simply tap or click one of the items displayed in the figure to activate their features. From left to right: 'Announcements' enable the teacher to communicate with the whole class. The 'Boards' show all of the publicly displayed content. The editable 'Members' feature can be viewed to be sure about the destination of a message; selecting 'Chat group' can show evidence of engagement with a debate about a topic. 'Settings' is best used to embed your page on a virtual learning environment or web page (you would do this by copying and pasting the embed code). The 'Analytics' provide very useful information about contributors and how long each has spent in your Learnium community. You will want to select the 'Moderation' icon to look for content that may have been flagged as inappropriate.

Learnium for assessment

This section will outline how Learnium's social learning features can be welcome assessment tools.

Synchronous and asynchronous communication via posting and chat

This could facilitate peer assessment or a more formalised peer review of work.

Collaboration on Word/Excel/PowerPoint files in real time

An essential component of such a piece of work would be an evaluation of each individual contribution.

Social features (likes, hashtags, mentions, feeds, notifications)

Sometimes the technology can get in the way of producing assessed work. The idea here is that learners will already be familiar with these features and behaviours. In addition, they could facilitate informal formative assessment in a similar way to sticky notes.

Learning analytics

This includes statistics on number of views and time spent reading. Data like this can make clear links between the time spent on assignments and the level of achievement. It could also help teachers reward effort.

Apps for Android, iPhone and the web

Learnium has been designed to be embedded into an LMS such as Canvas. There is also a learning app for both Android and IOS.

Learnium for learning

This section will link Learnium's rationale with the behaviours of 'social natives' (Foulger, 2014; Atherton, 2017). The thinking behind Learnium is that learners are likely to devote more time to their studies if their work is channelled through a network with which they are engaged. Learnium's construction mirrors that of a social network in the following ways.

- It encourages connections between users.

- Users can share posts and updates or ask each other questions.

- Content can be organised and made discoverable by the use of hashtags.

- People can be tagged, using @theirname.

Robert Dragan, Learnium's chief executive officer and co-founder, listed some principles that guide their development process.

- Keep it simple.

- Engage learners.

- Give teachers intuitive data (Dragan, 2017).

Learnium and social natives

Despite their innovative approach to learning, you may encounter resistance to wholesale adoption of systems like Learnium. Perhaps one of the reasons for this could be that the landscape of the social native is somewhat uncharted. For Foulger (2014), social natives create content that they then share, remix and reinterpret.

We could view this group as 'always on' but limited in their conscious understanding of what they are doing (Foulger, 2014; Atherton, 2017). If that is the case, there may be a risk that learners could be engaged in doing but not learning. By contrast, Learnium may have grasped the essence of how social natives learn. Social communication – and therefore social learning – produces overlapping associations in the same way as the human brain (Jones, 2012). Furthermore, Learnium plugs into the notion that social natives benefit from the instant, and potentially 24/7, sharing and feedback from their peers. Levy refers to this as *collective intelligence* (Levy, 1997, cited in Jones, 2012).

Links to the Teachers' Standards

S1: Set high expectations which inspire, motivate and challenge pupils

Learners could be closer to their peers than any other learning platform. This will necessitate a great deal of contracting and reinforcement.

S2: Promote good progress and outcomes by pupils

This requirement to guide learners to reflect on their progress and needs can be aided by their peers.

S3: Demonstrate good subject and curriculum knowledge

The immersive nature of Learnium presents opportunities for deep engagement in your subject.

S4: Plan and teach well-structured lessons

Learnium is designed to increase engagement and make lessons more varied.

S5: Adapt to the strengths and needs of all pupils

Learnium's breadth of experience offers the chance to differentiate by grouping, resources and pace.

S6: Make accurate and productive use of assessment

Learnium provides varied and stimulating ways to peer review, self-assess and assess both formally and informally.

S7: Manage behaviour effectively to ensure a good and safe environment

Stimulating, engaging resources and activities help build and maintain good student-teacher relationships.

S8: Fulfil wider professional responsibilities

Learnium is innovative in many ways, especially pedagogically. Your colleagues would be impressed with you.

References

Atherton, P (2017) *Kahoot for Assessment*. Liverpool: Kindle. Available online at: https://www.amazon.co.uk/Using-Kahoot-Assessment-teachers-learners-ebook/dp/B071CJSTC4/ref=sr_1_1?ie=UTF8&qid=1492696884&sr=8-1&keywords=pete+atherton [accessed 20 April 2017].

Dragan, R (2017) Interview with Robert Dragan (over Skype).

Foulger, M (2014) Meet the first generation of social natives. *Hootsuite Social Media Management*. https://blog.hootsuite.com/social-natives/. Web. 24 April 2017.

Jones, R (2012) *Understanding Digital Literacies: A Practical Introduction*. London: Routledge.

Video and audio tools

25
H5P

What is H5P?

This diverse video platform enables basic editing of online videos and the sharing and curating of creative, interactive content. H5P is a free, open-source platform that can be accessed via a plugin on WordPress or Drupal websites or through Moodle.

Perhaps of most interest is the option to edit videos sourced from YouTube and elsewhere.

As the edtech embraces the sharing economy through lightweight, open-source online content, there is now a proliferation of interactive video platforms, for example, Tuition Kit and EDpuzzle.

What can H5P do for teachers and learners?

For teachers

H5P content can be embedded seamlessly as HTML5 content on Moodle or Canvas. This means that you can direct your learners to Moodle or Canvas so they can complete quizzes, games, interactive videos, presentations and more.

Interactive video

This feature can be used as part of a flipped classroom or as a one-to-one classroom activity (flipped learning is discussed in a separate chapter).

Create interactive presentations

If you prefer breathing life into your lessons (rather than killing by PowerPoint), you may wish to try the Course Presentation tool. These presentations can incorporate any of H5P's features, such as interactive videos and assessed questions.

Teachers can also use visual images to help them pose high-order questions, to be assessed offline. One example of this is the Image Juxtaposition tool, which can show a 'before and after' scenario to provoke debate or develop reasoning or logical or creative thinking.

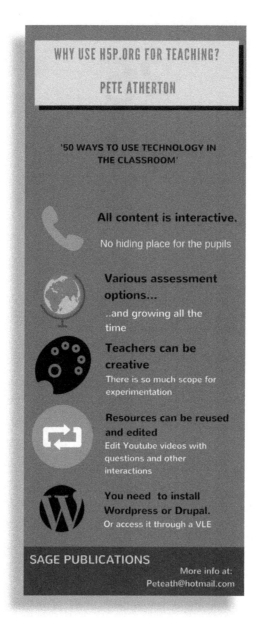

Image 25.1 Infographic: benefits of using H5P

For learners

H5P's main appeal will be the variety of tasks available. If the teacher uses H5P to plan a term's teaching, the learners could participate in a different H5P activity most days. One day they could take a personality test to determine what type of berry they are. On another they could be gauging their prior knowledge through an online questionnaire.

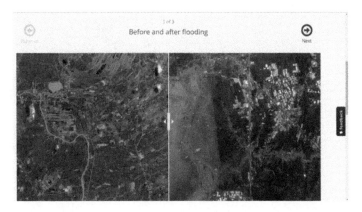

Image 25.2 After the flood: juxtaposition tool

Not only will the activities be user-friendly, they will be native to the platform to which their teacher has directed them. Learners can work on any device; some activities can be completed in their bedrooms, some on a tablet in school. Some will be learner-centred and collaborative, others teacher-centred and competitive.

How to use H5P

WordPress is simply a piece of free software for website building. All my websites, including **http://edtechblogs.com**, are built on WordPress. Chapter 37 summarises how to install and edit WordPress websites.

Add the H5P plugin

Sign in to your WordPress site and access the dashboard. I did this by typing **http://edtechblogs. com/wp-admin**, then entering my username and password. The dashboard reveals a menu on the left-hand sidebar. Roll over 'plugins', then 'add a new plugin'. Search for H5P content, then 'install now'. You will then need to activate the plugin before accessing its many features.

There are more features than can be accommodated into this chapter, for example, drag and drop. It may be helpful, however, to discuss one in depth. The interactive video editor is discussed below.

H5P for assessment

H5P are soon planning to launch a summative assessment function, boasting sophisticated analytics.

At the time of writing, there were around 35 categories of content on H5P. There is not enough space to discuss all of them in this chapter but the image below (25.3) shows a summary of potentially useful ways to use H5P to assess your learners.

Image 25.3 The growing range of options on H5P

Quiz questions

There are several options here, all of which display instant results:

- image juxtaposition;
- speak the words;
- drag the words;
- arithmetic quiz;
- interactive videos.

H5P for learning

H5P can be used by teachers in a 'command-style' session, where the teacher is the focal point and all learners are directed to look at the whiteboard (Mosston, 2002, cited in Capel et al., 2009). It is also useful for more learner-centred and less rigidly structured 'guided discovery' learning (Lee, 2010). Perhaps the most powerful weapon in its arsenal may be its compatibility with individualised, one-to-one (or 1:1) learning.

1:1 learning

1:1 learning is characterised by learners being issued with tablets or laptops and completing tasks paperlessly. Bocconi et al. (2013) found that the uptake of 1:1 learning had gathered momentum considerably in the 2010s. The geographical distribution, though, shows some marked differences in attitudes towards these new ways of learning. For instance, all of Norway's 180,000 upper secondary children have been issued with laptops (Bocconi et al., 2013; Svein Tore, 2017). In the UK, the figure was closer to 42,000 children, in a country with a population of 65 million, compared to Norway's 5 million.

Part of H5P's *raison d'être* is the spread of 1:1 learning, but this will always have to be balanced against the need to develop traditional literacies alongside new ones.

Links to the Teachers' Standards

S1: Set high expectations which inspire, motivate and challenge pupils

1:1 learning requires strict contracting and clarification of acceptable conduct.

S2: Promote good progress and outcomes by pupils

The numerous presentation, game and assessment tools can be rich and varied ways to develop prior knowledge.

S4: Plan and teach well-structured lessons

There are so many accessible and thought-provoking ways to use H5P. Examples of these are the image juxtaposition tool and the drag and drop functions. Also the 'agamotto' feature reveals layers of maps, rocks, film sets and so on to stimulate thought and debate.

There are many opportunities to flip the classroom with H5P – for example, the interactive quizzes and videos.

The questionnaires can capture learners' confidence or understanding. They can also provide feedback on enjoyment of activities.

The resources are easy to use and visually engaging. The interactive videos let you overlay images, links, text and more.

S5: Adapt to the strengths and needs of all pupils

The sheer variety of activities allows for multiple extension tasks, some of which can be collaborative. The many ways that teachers can ask questions (for example, dialogue cards or arithmetic quizzes) encourage teachers to be in control of their levels of scaffolding.

S6: Make accurate and productive use of assessment

The quizzes collate and reveal instant results, which can be powerful formative assessment tools. The documentation tool can be an innovative way for learners to self-assess and evaluate as a group.

References

Bocconi, S, Kampylis, P, Punie, Y (2013) Framing ICT-enabled innovation for learning: the case of one-to-one learning initiatives in Europe. *European Journal of Education*, 48(1): 113–130. Available online at: http://onlinelibrary.wiley.com/doi/10.1111/ejed.12021/pdf [accessed 23 May 2017].

Capel, S, Leask, M, Younie, S (2009) *Learning to Teach in the Secondary School*. London: Routledge.

Lee, HK (2010) *Faith-Based Education That Constructs*. Eugene, OR: Wipf & Stock.

Svein-Tore, G (2017) *Interview With Svein-Tore Griff Over Skype*.

26
YouTube

What is YouTube?

This book will make the bold assumption that the readers will already be familiar with YouTube.

As you may be very aware, YouTube has grown from a humble video-sharing site to a major force in media communication, since its inception in 2005. In terms of its pedagogical value, its potential is so vast that this chapter cannot explore individual educational YouTubers in depth. Instead, we will focus on its potential to help teachers supervise assessed work.

What can YouTube do for teachers and learners?

For teachers

Introduce a little levity into the classroom

Handle this advice with care! YouTube videos can be deployed as a lightweight framing device for a heavy topic. They are also useful as a starter activity to hook the learners and make them think or as stimulus material when the learners enter the class.

Flipping the classroom

Chapter 3 on the flipped classroom interrogates the benefits and limitations of this. Put simply, flipping the classroom means asking your learners to prepare for a lesson in advance by studying online resources. These resources are usually on video. The lesson is then devoted to analysis, debate, evaluation, hypothesis – all of which help develop high-order thinking skills. For example, Mark Glynn (see Image 26.2) makes videos about edtech, both for his university and his personal blog.

Store videos of lectures, activities, presentations or events

Video is notoriously data-heavy and can really slow down your computer, even your institution's server. YouTube videos are easily embeddable into websites and virtual learning environments – this will be discussed in the section on 'How to use YouTube for educational purposes', below.

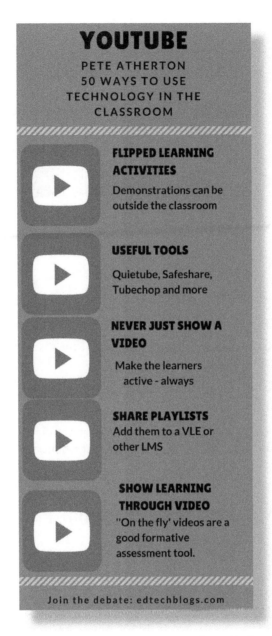

Image 26.1 Infographic: benefits of YouTube for learning

Tools

TubeChop, Quietube and SafeShare

Chop the most pertinent part of a video with TubeChop, and watch videos without distractions with Quietube and SafeShare.tv or SafeShare.

Image 26.2 Do you have the confidence to start your own channel?
Image reproduced by permission

For learners

It is native to their own consumption

Learners are likely to use YouTube for a significant part of their screen time. For that reason, it should feel comfortable and engaging for them.

Playlists can be used for homework

Learners could be asked to create their own playlists on a given topic. This could be an extension task, part of a research assignment or the start of a task that requires the class to curate, present or critique their playlists.

How to use YouTube for educational purposes

Create playlists

From your channel page, click 'create playlist'. When you or your learners see a video that helps them learn, they can then save it to their playlist, so it is easy to find.

Upload

The upload button is found in the top right of the screen. Your video can be listed as public, private or unlisted. After you have done that, upload a video file from your phone, tablet or PC.

Tag and share

Your video will need to be discoverable and searchable. To do this, search for your topic in YouTube's search bar. You can find the tags that are likely to rank the highest for your chosen topic.

YouTube for assessment

Demonstrate learning through creating a video

Ask learners to explain the contents of a muted video, as a group task, a silent debate or a micro presentation.

Digi essay

A digital essay requires learners to compose and record a short script. They would then find relevant Creative Commons-licensed images and add them to the audio. The videos can be peer-assessed through user comments, re-edited, then assessed by the teacher.

YouTube for learning

As a digital immigrant (Prensky, 2001), I sometimes fear for the effects of spending so much time squinting into an electronic device, head bowed. Generation AO – or 'always on' (Foulger, 2014) – seem to have collapsed the distinction between work and leisure, between learning and living. In the 'always on' digital world, then, living *is* learning. It is also sharing (Foulger, 2014). People's predilection for being self-taught is gathering apace, as informal learning exists both alongside and outside school (Lange, 2016).

One frequently used approach to flipping the classroom with YouTube is *just in time learning* (Simkins and Maier, 2010). Here, learners are directed to some video content a few hours before class. They are required to answer questions through a virtual learning environment or another appropriate content management system. These questions could also be answered through a closed Facebook group or a Twitter hashtag.

If the flipped classroom is truly part of a *paradigm shift,* in which elearning is naturally woven into the fabric of learning (Scheg, 2015), YouTube's status is safe for now, as where else can teachers source, share and store video with such ease and security?

Links to the Teachers' Standards

S1: Set high expectations which inspire, motivate and challenge pupils

Use of and engagement through YouTube necessitate a great deal of contracting in terms of ethics and appropriate behaviour.

S2: Promote good progress and outcomes by pupils

The flipped classroom (particularly the 'just in time' learning approach) can be a powerful way to develop prior knowledge. It can also help address misunderstandings (S3a).

(Continued)

(Continued)

S5: Adapt to the strengths and needs of all pupils

Using YouTube for independent learning can help learners scaffold knowledge with autonomy.

If the emphasis is on learners doing something with the video content, they will be doing a great deal more than merely watching.

S6d: Give pupils regular feedback, both orally and through accurate marking, and encourage pupils to respond to the feedback

Making digi essays or short videos helps check understanding. If the focus is on understanding, not filming and editing, those videos can be reshot and edited in response to the feedback.

S8: Fulfil wider professional responsibilities

A successful YouTube channel can be very good public relations for the institution and create some welcome engagement from parents and the wider community.

References

Foulger, M (2014) Meet the first generation of social natives. *Hootsuite*. Web. 10 August 2017.

Lange, PG (2016) *Kids on YouTube*. Walnut Creek, CA: Left Coast Press.

Prensky, M (2001) Digital natives, digital immigrants, part II. Do they really think differently? *On the Horizon*, 9(5): 1–6.

Scheg, A (2015) *Implementation and Critical Assessment of the Flipped Classroom Experience*, 1st edition. Hershey, PA: Information Science Reference.

Simkins, S, Maier, M (2010) *Just-in-Time Teaching*. Sterling, VA: Stylus.

27

EDpuzzle

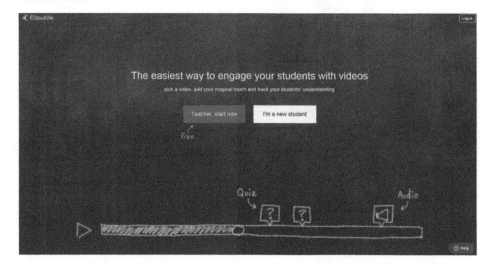

Image 27.1 No hiding place for students! EDpuzzle

What is EDpuzzle?

If you've been looking for ways to use video-based activities in the classroom but are concerned about not assessing your learners, EDpuzzle – a video presentation tool – could be worth a try. As denoted by the illustration on the landing page, EDpuzzle enables teachers to edit videos sourced from a variety of channels, for example YouTube, Vimeo, Ted Talks and National Geographic – amongst others. The videos can be automatically paused to reveal questions for the learners to answer. There is also the option to add audio – for example, a recording of the teacher asking a question. Not only can video help assess, EDpuzzle allows you to track your learners' progress and generate data on their achievement.

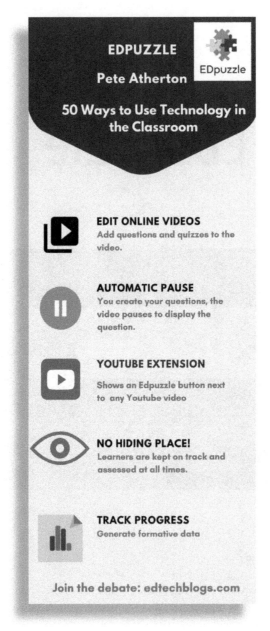

Image 27.2 Infographic: benefits of using EDpuzzle

What can EDpuzzle do for teachers and learners?

For teachers

The most alluring feature that EDpuzzle has is that it creates a situation where there is no hiding place for the learners. If you show a video, the learners will know that they are required to pay attention because, in a minute or so, there will be a question, the answer to which will be assessed.

You can either source a video from the significant range of channels or upload your own. Part of the skill of using EDpuzzle will be entering specific, targeted search terms. Once you find a suitable video, you are then asked if you want to use it. Using the video gives you the opportunity to edit it, by cropping to eliminate any extraneous detail, or by adding questions and/or audio. EDpuzzle has created videos and PowerPoints to provide tutorials on how to use the platform.

For learners

EDpuzzle's features can provide a great deal of autonomy to learners. For extension tasks, flipped learning and good old homework, students can create and upload their own videos and evaluate, analyse, critique or provide comments on them. In a flipped classroom, they can add images, links or equations to questions. If the learners answer at home, the teacher can monitor viewing history and quiz results. The teacher can prevent the class from skipping the video, so they will be forced to watch it all the way through.

How to use EDpuzzle

To add questions, you click on the question mark icon entitled 'Quizzes'. This then gives you three options: open-ended questions, multiple choice and comments.

Integrating with Google Classroom

Once logged in, learners can join a classroom in one of the following ways:

- by clicking on a link;
- by entering a code in their account.

Teachers can import a class from Google Classroom. There is a chapter dedicated to G Suite, part of which concerns Google Classroom.

EDpuzzle for assessment

EDpuzzle's main strengths here are its emphasis on clear assessment and the creation and monitoring of data. The teacher could host quizzes as a diagnostic test or ask open-ended questions to be answered in pairs on a worksheet or in a workbook. You could also consider the varieties of assessment options below.

Oral assessment

EDpuzzle gives teachers opportunities to prepare and rehearse their questioning techniques. As it provides the choice of open questions, comments and closed, multiple-choice questions, EDpuzzle could signpost to teachers how useful it can be to prepare questions in advance.

Peer assessment

If learners are put into pairs in a classroom or as part of a virtual learning group, this could open up some opportunities for powerful peer assessment.

Ipsative assessment

The notion of encouraging learners to beat their personal best could identify and evaluate the skills and behaviours that led to the learner's previous highest score.

EDpuzzle for learning

Self-assessment

Learners can use EDpuzzle to self-assess, either at home or in school. Though self-assessment's benefits are often doubted, its effectiveness is attributed to how it fosters self-regulation (Wiliam, 2011). When learning is self-regulated, learners can bring together their thinking, actions and emotions (Wiliam, 2011). Mega et al. (2013) demonstrated there is a correlation between the influence of self-regulated learning and motivation.

Metacognition (or thinking about thinking)

When learners answer a question posed through EDpuzzle, will you ask them to share why they answered in this way and what alternative answers could also be feasible? Doing this is likely to improve their 'intrinsic motivation' and feeling of control over their decisions (Deci and Ryan, 2008, cited in Dron and Anderson, 2015). Baumeister et al. (2015), however, warned against confusing intense feeling with intense learning. Furthermore, perhaps we should be wary of the influence of psychology on educational theory and practice.

Links to the Teachers' Standards

S1: Set high expectations which inspire, motivate and challenge pupils

A lot of the stretch and challenge could be derived from the rich questioning that you plan to supplement the questions that you set on the video.

S2: Promote good progress and outcomes by pupils

As a flipped activity, your EDpuzzle could also contain links to further reading to build on prior knowledge. You could also insist that learners reflect on what they learned and how.

S3: Demonstrate good subject and curriculum knowledge

Your sessions could find ways to address spelling, punctuation and grammar in the learners' answers. 'Reach' or stretch questions could help promote the value of scholarship.

S4: Plan and teach well-structured lessons

The fact that videos will be paused for various question types is likely to punctuate your lessons to allow for thinking and assessment.

S5: Adapt to the strengths and needs of all pupils

As EDpuzzle activities can be completed wherever there is an internet connection, there is no reason for anyone to be left behind. The varied question types (multiple-choice, open) also help support all abilities.

S6: Make accurate and productive use of assessment

Formative assessment is integral to the appeal of EDpuzzle and the premium option also offers analytics.

S7: Manage behaviour effectively to ensure a good and safe environment

It will be clear that all learners are expected to be on task and active at all times.

References

Baumeister, RF, Alquist, JL, Vohs, KD (2015) *Illusions of Learning: Irrelevant Emotions Inflate Judgements of Learning*. Available online at: http://onlinelibrary.wiley.com/doi/10.1002/bdm.1836/abstract [accessed 15 August 2017].

Dron, J, Anderson, T (2015) *Teaching Crowds: Learning and Social Media*. Edmonton, AB: AU Press.

Mega, C, Ronconi, L, De Beni, R (2013) What makes a good student? How emotions, self-regulated learning, and motivation contribute to academic achievement. *Journal of Educational Psychology*, 106: 121–131.

Wiliam, D (2011) *Embedded Formative Assessment*. Bloomington, IN: Solution Tree.

28

TuitionKit

Image 28.1

What is TuitionKit?

At the time of writing, TuitionKit defines itself as 'your ultimate learning tool'. Teachers and students can register free and use for 3 days without charge. For £4.99 a month, subscribers can access thousands of educational videos and add questions to their own videos (like EDpuzzle and H5P). The focus is on maths, science and English at secondary level and the content is designed to match that of the major UK exam board syllabuses.

What can TuitionKit do for teachers and learners?

For teachers

There are thousands of English, maths and science videos which could be effective supplementary materials for a virtual learning environment or as part of a flipped classroom. As teachers can add their own questions, this also opens up possibilities for varied in-class activities.

'The best of YouTube' helps teachers navigate their way to relevant content.

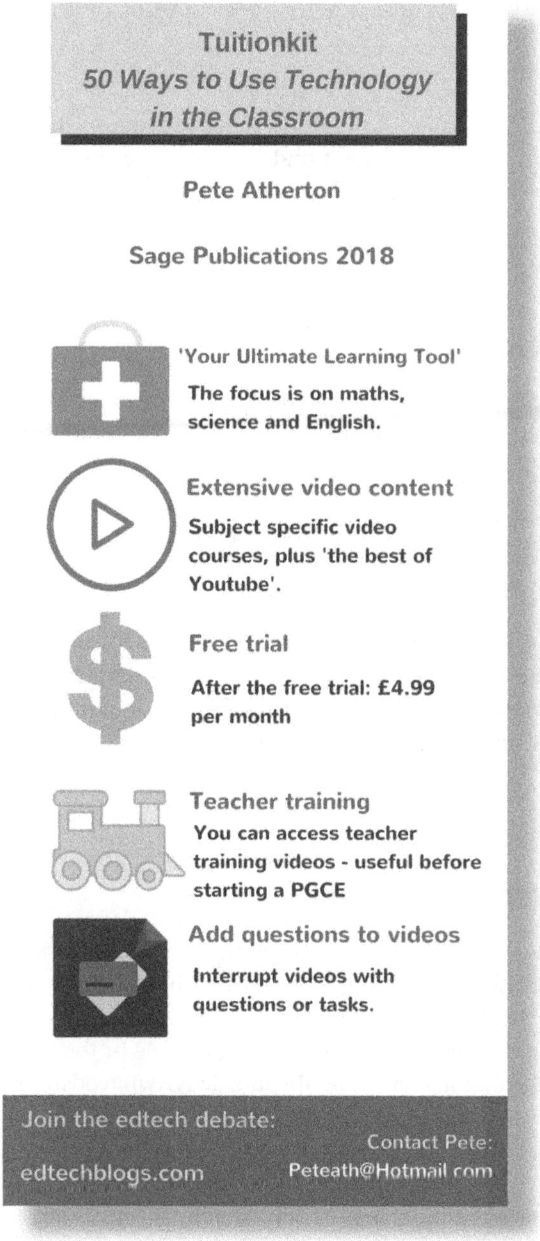

Image 28.2 Infographic: benefits of using TuitionKit

Teacher training

This section hosts scores of videos to help trainees with issues from teaching principles, behaviour management and the psychology of teaching to reviewing lessons, lesson activities and how students learn.

For learners

Flipping the classroom

One of the most appealing features of flipped learning activities is the way that learners can pause and rewind at their own pace if they don't understand or become distracted. TuitionKit augments this by enabling learners to add or review notes on each section.

How to use TuitionKit

Import videos from YouTube

There are three ways to import videos from YouTube: by video, by channel or by playlist. Each of these options can be completed by copying and pasting the web address into the box provided.

TuitionKit for assessment

Creating a video event

In a similar way to video-based tools like EDpuzzle, TuitionKit enables teachers to interrupt videos by adding questions. The way to create a 'video event' is to roll over the icons displayed in the right-hand sidebar. These icons represent the options to review or add notes, mark as watch later, add notes or worksheets and create a new audio or video event.

TuitionKit for learning

The flipped mastery classroom

TuitionKit could be used in a more asynchronous, personalised way to help develop mastery. Bergmann and Sams (2012) develop the notion of the flipped classroom by proposing the *flipped mastery classroom*. Learning this way encourages learners to work on different activities at different times and sometimes in different spaces. One learner may be in the library attempting to master a single problem. A small group may be using the interactive whiteboard to answer some of the questions from a video on TuitionKit (Bergmann and Sams, 2012). The role of the teacher is initially to diagnose which learners need to conduct practical work, who needs to take a test and who needs support. Once these have been established, the teacher takes on the role of a *guide on the side* (Scheg, 2015). This would complement the Carter Review's emphasis on mastery learning (Carter, 2015).

One of the enduring risks of being too evangelical about any emerging technologies is of becoming distracted from persistent issues in education. The way this could happen is by investing time and money into educational technology and this distracting schools and learner from what really needs to change. Hattie (2015) calls this the *politics of distraction*. One symptom of this is the idea that schools are using technology as a new way to consume knowledge, instead as a portal to the creation of enhanced knowledge (Hattie, 2015). To develop Ingle and Duckworth's (2013) work on the emerging 'multimodal literacies' of the digital learning experience, TuitionKit's challenge will be like any other edtech platform: to ensure that it is empowering through the adoption of varied but complementary literacies.

Links to the Teachers' Standards

S1: Set high expectations which inspire, motivate and challenge pupils

If the 'flipped mastery' approach is employed, learners will need to be briefed on acceptable conduct and health and safety. The bank of resources and teachers' own video courses can stretch and challenge.

S2: Promote good progress and outcomes by pupils

Some aspects of the site are gamified insofar as learners can earn badges for how many videos they watch. The key for teachers will be matching this to evidence of learning.

S4: Plan and teach well-structured lessons

Flipping the classroom frees up the lesson for more engaging learning experiences.

S5: Adapt to the strengths and needs of all pupils

The 'tracking students' progress' feature enables teachers to analyse the videos watched and questions answered by each learner. This should help teachers see the support they give to learners as an ongoing process.

S6: Make accurate and productive use of assessment

'Student/teacher conversations' allow teachers to ask learners questions about their work and for learners to ask for help.

References

Bergmann, J, Sams, A (2012) *Flip Your Classroom: Reach Every Student in Every Class Every Day*. Washington: International Society for Technology in Education.

Carter, A (2015) *Carter Review of Initial Teacher Training (ITT)*. Available online at: https://www.gov.uk/government/uploads/system/uploads/attachment_data/file/399957/Carter_Review.pdf [accessed 20 October 2016].

Hattie, J (2015) *What Doesn't Work in Education: The Politics of Distraction*. London: Pearson.

Ingle, S, Duckworth, V (2013) *Enhancing Learning Through Technology in Lifelong Learning: Fresh Ideas, Innovative Strategies*. Berkshire: Open University Press, pp27–28.

Scheg, A (2015) *Implementation and Critical Assessment of the Flipped Classroom Experience*. Hershey, PA: Information Science Reference.

29
Panopto

What is Panopto?

As a video presentation and teaching platform, Panopto has a suitably slick and user-friendly interface. Prior to summarising Panopto's features, it may be prudent to point out that this is a paid service.

The platform enables educators to film themselves, capture the content of their screens and mix a video of a presentation with other online content. Panopto is largely used in universities but more primary and secondary teachers are starting to use it too.

What can Panopto do for teachers and learners?

For teachers

Panopto can make planning more seamless and enjoyable, as the video presentations will be formed by viewing attractive and powerful learning resources. Especially if used as part of a flipped classroom, it minimises the need for the didactic 'command' style of teaching (Mosston and Ashworth, 1990).

Micro lectures

Panopto is intended to be integrated seamlessly into an institution's learning management system. This can be achieved by embedding video content.

Lecture capture

Teachers can record and store an orderly set of lectures and presentations. These could be a recording of a lecture or designed as video content to be viewed outside the classroom.

Video content management

The videos can form part of a clear and coherent course.

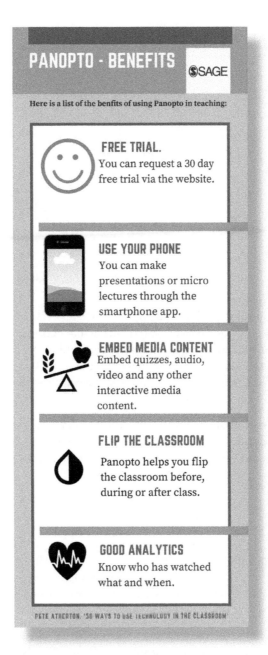

Image 29.1 Infographic: benefits of using Panopto

For learners

Panopto's flipped classroom approach encourages learners to work at their own speed, as they can pause and rewind, even interact with pools and quizzes. This is discussed in greater depth in the section entitled, 'Panopto for learning', below.

How to use Panopto

Image 29.2 Not just for universities . . .

Firstly, you need to download the software, then decide whether you want to record your computer screen or record yourself presenting. Once you have made that decision, click the red record button. Though that may appear straightforward, you may want to think carefully about the lighting, the position and quality of the camera and microphone. Indeed, it is essential to trial your video presentations many times before releasing them. Also, test them with a colleague before allowing your students access.

More ambitious teachers may want to experiment with the more ostentatious multi-camera recordings. This feature lets you capture your presentation or lecture from several angles, plus the content of your screen. You can even capture and record content from your phone, for example, a close-up of a flip chart or an object.

Panopto for assessment

Panopto produce analytics that reveal which learners viewed each video and for how long. This data can also show the point at which each learner exited the video and which part of the video engaged them most. In that respect, Panopto is more of a learner surveillance mechanism than an assessment tool.

That said, Panopto have some interactive tools to help teachers pose questions during video playback and these can be integrated into your learning management system. The section below also details some more ideas that would be useful for formative assessment.

Panopto for learning

Panopto can be used as part of a flipped classroom in numerous ways that make it more likely that activities during lessons will be enhanced by the teacher (Bergmann and Sams, 2012).

A discussion-orientated flipped classroom

Learners are asked to view a selection of videos around a theme that will be relevant to the day's lesson (Riddell, 2012). The class time is spent debating these issues, maybe as a Socratic seminar, where learners are assigned to study the video content, then bring with them a relevant question that cannot be answered with either 'yes' or 'no' (Young and Moran, 2017).

A group-based flipped classroom

This method again requires the learners to study online resources beforehand. When they come to class, they are given a series of problems or challenges to work on in groups. This is a similar type of peer instruction to one witnessed by Quim Sabria from Edpuzzle (Social Media and Edtech, 2017), in which groups in a school in California were organised into 'rotation zones'. These zones would ask each other why they had answered the way that they did and could only rotate after mastering each task.

Links to the Teachers' Standards

S2: Promote good progress and outcomes by pupils

Whether you use the flipped or traditional classroom model, Panopto allows the freedom and flexibility to meet this Standard.

S5: Adapt to the strengths and needs of all pupils

You could ensure that your videos offer significant scaffolding and immersive extension tasks.

S8: Fulfil wider professional responsibilities

The videos you create will look impressive and this will help promote the expertise, professionalism and innovativeness of your department.

References

Bergmann, J, Sams, A (2012) *Flip Your Classroom: Reach Every Student in Every Class Every Day*. International Society for Technology in Education/ISTE.

Mosston, M, Ashworth, S (1990) *The Spectrum of Teaching Styles*. New York: Longman.

Riddell, R (2012) *16 Flipped Learning Uses in K-12 and College Classrooms*. Available online at: http://www.educationdive.com/news/16-flipped-learning-uses-in-k-12-and-college-classrooms/74311/ [accessed 13 April 2017].

Social Media and Edtech (2017) *Interview with Quim Sabria*. 1. 12 April 2017. Available online at: http://edtechblogs.com [accessed 20 April 2017].

Young, C, Moran, C (2017) *Applying the Flipped Classroom Model to English Language Arts Education*. Hershey, PA: Information Science Reference.

30

Podcasting: Audacity and GarageBand

What is podcasting?

A podcast is essentially a radio show but in edtech terms it is much more than that. The word 'podcast' is a *portmanteau* word, which combines the brand name 'iPod' with 'broadcast' (compare with Instagram as a *portmanteau* word). In the early noughties, it became possible to have updates of audio content sent directly to a portable media player, an example of which was an iPod.

In the late 2010s, podcasts gathered momentum, as they became easier to produce. They also became more appealing to consumers, as they could be downloaded on to smartphones and played in cars. This chapter will evaluate two ways to podcast. The first will be by using GarageBand, which is a Mac-only program, and Audacity, which is free, open-source software and accessible through any operating system.

What can podcasting do for teachers and learners?

For teachers

However your curriculum is structured, podcasts are likely to raise the profile of both you and your department. Whether you use Audacity or GarageBand, there are several ways in which podcasting does this:

- by creating quantitative data on number of downloads and shares;

- by sharing your personality and professionalism with colleagues, managers and stakeholders;

- by effectively giving your department a brand identity, which is likely to encourage a deeper level of learner engagement.

Image 30.1 Infographic: benefits of podcasting

For learners

If you trust your learners, you may feel that they could develop enough technical and social skills and maturity to present their own shows, even their own radio station. Podcasting can be a powerful way to develop collaborative and communication skills. There is also the possibility that learners may become niche celebrities, as young consumers are inured in a celebrity culture where there is room for ordinary people (Marshall and Redmond, 2015).

How to Podcast

GarageBand

Mac users will already have GarageBand and a built-in microphone on their computers or MacBooks.

The GarageBand app can also be installed on any iOS device. Once the program is open, select 'New project', then 'Podcast'. You can either record everything live or as separate tracks. If you want to learn to edit with sophistication, this will take a little time but can be learned through YouTubers like Tim Ferriss (you can also search for 'GarageBand tutorial').

Audacity

Audacity is, perhaps, more accessible and user-friendly than GarageBand. Once you have located your internal microphone or attached an external one, you should be ready to record by clicking the red 'record' button. Your audio file must be in MP3 format and this requires a MP3 decoder called LAME, which you can download from Buanzo.org. Again, for a more granular grasp of audio editing, seek out YouTubers such as Radio.co.

A hosting service like Libsyn would be advisable. If you use WordPress, the 'Powerpress' plugin will host your podcast through Bluebrry and create the rich site summary (RSS) feed, which you will then copy and paste into iTunes. RSS feeds enable people to access your podcast. If you do not use WordPress, try accessing your RSS feed through Feedburner. When you have pasted the RSS feed of your podcast into iTunes, your podcast will then be available all over the world!

For a simple 'how to' guide to RSS feeds and iTunes, watch Technologyguru on YouTube; search for 'How to submit a podcast to iTunes'.

Podcasting for assessment

Much of the literature discusses the use of podcasts to assess at higher education level (Hopkins, 2012). However, there is evidence that podcasts can also help assess secondary learners. Maths and science pupils can use podcasts to show how they solved a problem. For any literacy task, podcasting can be an effective way to differentiate the class; some learners will feel that planning their ideas on paper is a little intimidating. Using a podcast to develop spoken language skills can have a dual function. For example, if learners were asked to record a dramatic monologue or an advert, they could be asked to also provide a draft and final script.

Podcasting for learning

Auditory learning

Some subjects lend themselves more to auditory learning. Modern foreign languages is one such example. In a successfully differentiated classroom, auditory learning could also be a powerful way for English as a second language and English as an additional language pupils to learn your subject through spoken English.

Learning outside the classroom

The real power of podcasts is their potential to engage learners outside the classroom. In that respect, they can form part of a *connectivist* learning experience, which embraces the notion that today's knowledge could be obsolete or incorrect by tomorrow (Siemens, 2005). If learners are directed to subscribe to relevant podcasts through iTunes or RSS feeds, they could begin to see learning as an immersive journey. A further application of podcasting could be to use the medium to create a *rhizomatic* learning culture, where learning has no beginning or end (Cormier, 2014).

Links to the Teachers' Standards

S1: Set high expectations which inspire, motivate and challenge pupils

Any activities that require learners to take and post photos require careful contracting. Pupils need to be briefed on the risks and implications of these in terms of health and safety, legality, ethics and safeguarding. This need to be responsible could also help evidence this Standard.

S2: Promote good progress and outcomes by pupils

Podcasts are searchable and easy to reference. This can help build prior knowledge, especially if students become attached to a specific podcast.

S5: Adapt to the strengths and needs of all pupils

Podcasting can be an inclusive way of enabling learners to get started on written assignments. If other learners feel more competent and confident with written tasks, they could research and write about existing podcasts in your subject.

S6: Make accurate and productive use of assessment

Presentations have long been a worthy method of formative assessment. Groups or individuals can summarise their findings from a small-scale research project or even build a collaborative response from which the whole class could revise.

S8: Fulfil wider professional responsibilities

Teachers could provide a monthly bulletin celebrating learners' achievements and summarising the content of the course. Selected learners could participate in this to showcase their knowledge, conduct interviews about their experiences or even do a party piece.

References

Cormier, D (2014) *Rhizomatic Education: Community as Curriculum – Dave's Educational Blog.* Davecormier.com. Available online at: http://davecormier.com/edblog/2008/06/03/rhizomatic-education-community-as-curriculum/ [accessed 13 April 2017].

Hopkins, E (2012) The potential value of student created podcasts as assessment tools in higher education. *Educationalfutures*. Available online at: http://educationstudies.org.uk/wp-content/uploads/2013/11/elizabeth_hopkins.pdf [accessed 12 April 2017].

Marshall, P, Redmond, S (2015) *A Companion to Celebrity*. Oxford: Taylor & Francis.

Siemens, G (2005) *Connectivism: A Learning Theory for the Digital Age*. Available online at: http://www.itdl.org/journal/jan_05/article01.htm [accessed 11 April 2017].

Collaborative working

31
Padlet

What is Padlet?

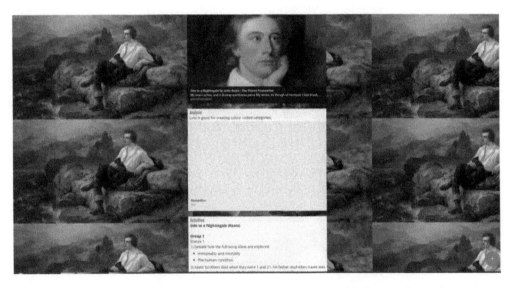

Image 31.1 Wall of death - one of my Padlets on romantic poetry

Padlet is a digital, collaborative canvas. Padlet was previously known as Wallwisher. Though Padlet works perfectly well as a website, it is also available as an iOS or Android app, a Chrome extension, a Chrome app or a WordPress plugin.

As its previous name suggests, Padlet allows users to create virtual 'walls'. These customisable 'walls' can contain text and links that embed web pages or video. These 'walls' can also store multimedia files. Padlet has been selected for its ease of use in terms of planning and classroom activities. It is also worth considering the ways in which Padlet can enable teachers to 'flip' the classroom.

Image 31.2 Infographic: benefits of using Padlet

What can Padlet do for teachers and learners?

For teachers: storage and organisation

Padlet makes it easy for teachers to store and display multiple documents and a wide range of multimedia content. Padlets can make it easy to display the following:

- lesson objectives;

- tasks;

- embedded videos;

- embedded websites;

- embedded images;

- embedded PowerPoints;

- additional reading on Word files;

- stretch and challenge activities;

- scaffolding: for example, a list of supplementary questions.

For learners

Brainstorm to create a bulletin board

- Students can use Padlet at the start of a topic to draw on their existing knowledge.

- They can provide feedback on their progress, or on a module or unit of work.

- Boards can chronicle events within a timeframe or related to a specific event.

Research, collect and display

- Padlet allows you to display worksheets and projects so that they are always accessible. One effective way of using these worksheets is to ask students to research a topic in groups. They could then present their findings or 'curate' them as part of a 'marketplace' activity.

How to use Padlet

To add content, select '+new', then double click or tap to add content. This content can be typed and augmented by adding an attachment; attachments can be a photo, video or PDF file. You can also record from your webcam.

Once completed, the work can be saved in several formats, for example, as an image or PDF. You can share your Padlet on social media, Google Play or in the App Store. It can also be embedded on to web pages or an institution's virtual learning environment (VLE). The way to do this is by exporting the document as HTML, then pasting the code on to the web page or VLE.

Settings

Before starting an activity, make sure that you have made a decision about what you want to permit your learners to do with the Padlet. Click 'Share', then 'People and privacy'. You can then decide if you want learners to be able to just read, write, moderate or administer. Providing administration rights does, of course, carry significant risks, so it may best be avoided.

Padlet for assessment

How are teachers going to ensure that all learners have made progress? How are they to assess that progress against clear and fair criteria? Here are some quick and easy ways to ensure that your students are providing evidence of progress:

- ranking to develop high-order thinking;

- building on previous knowledge.

Self-assessment

Padlet walls can be effective ways to gather learner feedback on their progress. This could be anonymous or not, depending on the visibility of the feedback and composition of the group.

A group essay/presentation

If learners are asked to display their names next to their posts, this introduces a degree of accountability to their work. As long as the criteria are transparent and achievable, the project can provide some useful formative assessment.

A plenary wall

This could focus on learners' achievement in the lesson. It could also be tied to meeting learning objectives or assessment outcomes.

Peer assessment

Once a Padlet has been created, learners can easily assess each other. If the teacher provides the criteria on paper first, learners can provide 'what went well' and 'even better if' comments next to each post.

At the time of writing, Padlet had plans to develop the platform so that premium users could create student reports or portfolios and record whether students have attempted a piece of work. This sophistication towards analytics will be a reaction to the need for teachers to create more transparent data. It will also give them a potential weapon against homework excuses from students, as teachers will be able to ascertain the last time that a student worked on a document. Another need to which the paid versions are responding is that of integration with Google apps and other more prominent educational networks like Edmodo.

Padlet for learning

There is a paucity of literature relating to comparing synchronous (or real-time) versus asynchronous learning in the secondary context, as much of the work concerns adult distance learning.

Flipping the classroom

The flipped classroom model is worth pursuing at this juncture, in order to illuminate the potential of Padlet in terms of pedagogy and assessment. If Padlet is used for flipped learning activities, this could reflect how education is moving away from a monolithic, mass-market model which was designed during the Victorian age. In this antiquated method, learners were seen as passive, empty vessels to be filled with information (Mezirow, 1978). The emerging 'free-range' model is more personalised, flexible, negotiable (Wheeler, 2012).

Links to the Teachers' Standards

S1: Set high expectations which inspire, motivate and challenge pupils

Using Padlet can foster the self-efficacy required to stretch and challenge. Working collaboratively and ensuring that learners' content is appropriate help teachers demonstrate positive attitudes.

S2: Promote good progress and outcomes by pupils

Padlets can help accommodate the miasma of learning styles in any given classroom. The way it does this is by building multimodal literacies.

S3: Demonstrate good subject and curriculum knowledge

Creating on Padlet feels organic: content is instantly saved but easily edited. This can build confidence and help address misconceptions.

S4: Plan and teach well-structured lessons

If homework can sometimes feel like a punishment for learners, flipped learning activities on Padlet can at least offer visually appealing ways to promote a love of learning and create an engaging curriculum.

S5: Adapt to the strengths and needs of all pupils

The fact that a Padlet is a blank canvas helps teachers demonstrate their skills in differentiating by content, process, final product and learners' interests and abilities.

S6: Make accurate and productive use of assessment

Padlet can help learners create assessed presentations. If the learners' settings allow editing, or list the teacher as a collaborator, it will be easy to provide and act on feedback.

S7: Manage behaviour effectively to ensure a good and safe environment

If you use Padlet in a flipped learning environment, there are fewer opportunities for learners to behave disruptively.

S8: Fulfil wider professional responsibilities

Remember, the resources that your learners produce are ways to market the institution and your own skill and professionalism.

References

Mezirow, J (1978) Perspective transformation. *Adult Education Quarterly*, 28(2): 100–110.

Wheeler, S (2012) *The Digital Classroom: Harnessing Technology for the Future of Learning and Teaching*, 2nd edition. London: David Fulton Publishers.

32

QR codes

Image 32.1 This is the QR code for my ebook about Kahoot!

What are QR codes?

QR codes (or quick response codes) are two-dimensional barcodes that link straight to online content when read by a QR code reader on a mobile device. QR codes may have lost some of the novelty that they had acquired at the start of the 2010s but they are still a versatile addition to the edtech arsenal. Indeed, one of the enduring themes of this book is that technology should not be a barrier to learning: novelty (or hostility) can be an example of a barrier.

What can QR codes do for teachers and learners?

For teachers

Teachers can avoid having to ask learners to type in a clunky URL by positioning QR codes on desks. The range of activities that can be accessed instantly can lead to varied and engaging lessons.

The teacher can set homework, extension tasks and flipped learning activities by displaying a code on the whiteboard or on a piece of paper. Teachers can create a more collaborative classroom culture

Image 32.2 Infographic: benefits of using QR codes

by asking learners to share their own creative work with their peers (Gasim, 2017). Examples of these could be:

- creative or informative videos;
- podcasts;

- infographics;

- cross-sections or diagrams;

- flowcharts or timelines;

- digital portfolios of creative work;

- summaries of solutions to problems.

QR codes also make it easy to gather feedback from learners or their parents. The learner feedback can be drawn from linking to SurveyMonkey, Bristol Online, Kahoot! Surveys or Google Forms. It could be a diagnostic tool for learners or even used for formative assessment. Parents could be surveyed for evaluative feedback at parents' evenings or at the end of term.

For learners

If a teacher provides QR codes to link to selected resources, they can offer immersive, challenging learning experiences while removing the need for learners to search through swathes of irrelevant content. An example of this could be music students whose sheet music also contains QR codes that take them to augmented reality learning resources, additional reading, performance footage, streaming music and so on (Kaschub and Smith, 2014).

There can be an element of serendipity introduced to learning though QR codes (this is discussed in more detail in the 'QR codes for learning' section, below). Learners can take part in treasure hunts, in which they are directed to strategically placed QR codes around a classroom, library, corridor, outdoor space, educational visit, event, blog or web page.

How to use QR codes

The first thing you will need to do will be to install a QR reader app on your phone or tablet. This will enable you to test the codes that you create.

Creating the QR code from a URL

Tools such as Snap.vu are there to help you generate QR codes from a URL. When the QR code has been created, simply print it out or display it on the whiteboard or on a collaborative document on Padlet or Google Drive, for example.

QR codes for assessment

QR codes are not assessment tools but can be deployed in some aforementioned ways, for example, as diagnostic tools, to link to surveys to gauge understanding, to link to assessment tools and to make it easier to peer-assess learners' online creations.

Differentiation

With a little planning beforehand, teachers can ensure that activities are differentiated by group-ings, by task and by outcome. The QR codes that can be placed on desks can be chosen to pair high, medium and low achievers together for support, offer advanced and extension tasks for high achievers and use pupil data to show that your planning is acting on your awareness of factors such as pupil premium, special educational needs and disabilities and English as an additional language. This data provides essential guidance on how to act on assessment information, therefore justifying differentiation (Tomlinson and Moon, 2013). A single A4 sheet can provide differentiated instruc-tions, all tied to a single QR code, which will link to those differentiated resources.

QR codes for learning

Traditional learning models are instructional and teacher-centred and operate within sometimes nar-row parameters (Huang et al., 2014). As education's forays into the digital age gather momentum, the notion of the 'connectivist' classroom appears increasingly apt. In that respect, QR codes match the desire for serendipity – the idea of taking pleasure in the seemingly accidental discovery of new knowledge. If learners can be encouraged to be the kernel of emerging, fluid knowledge (Siemens, 2005; Friesen and Lowe, 2012), then the real power of QR codes could be in learners creating, shar-ing and updating existing and emerging knowledge.

There must always be a note of caution here: the essential challenge is to avoid using teaching with technology as opposed to empowering people to learn through technology. More crucially, QR codes must never be used to reframe tired and outdated pedagogies (Blin and Munro, 2008, cited in Kirkwood and Price, 2014).

Links to the Teachers' Standards

S1: Set high expectations which inspire, motivate and challenge pupils

QR codes lend themselves to extension tasks, which can be placed in a multitude of locations.

S2: Promote good progress and outcomes by pupils

QR codes can be used in a variety of ways and this can help teachers show knowledge and under-standing of how students learn.

S3: Demonstrate good subject and curriculum knowledge

QR codes can be used to provide swift links to others' resources. This can help teachers show a critical understanding of developments in their subject area, without having to prepare volumi-nous resources.

S4: Plan and teach well-structured lessons

You can stimulate intellectual curiosity by using QR codes to make knowledge feel more spontaneous, discoverable, personalised.

S5: Adapt to the strengths and needs of all pupils

Your selection of QR codes for individuals or groups can be an efficient way to show that you are differentiating or, more crucially, catering for all learning needs.

S6: Make accurate and productive use of assessment

QR codes can be used to link to a summary of 'what went well' and 'even better if', that has been generated by the teacher or through self or peer assessment.

S8: Fulfil wider professional responsibilities

Student work can be celebrated and their achievements publicised by adding a series of QR codes to open evenings, parents' evenings and other events.

References

Friesen, N, Lowe, S (2012) *The Questionable Promise of Social Media for Education: Connective Learning and the Commercial Imperative*. Available online at: https://www.researchgate.net/profile/Norm_Friesen/publication/263490296_The_questionable_promise_of_social_media_for_education_connective_learning_and_the_commercial_imperative/links/54c573f00cf256ed5a9b0a4f.pdf [accessed 8 January 2016].

Gasim, F (2017) *Infographics – EdTechReview (ETR)*. Edtechreview.in. Available online at: http://edtechreview.in/resources/infographics [accessed 2 June 2017].

Huang, L, Bhayani, R, Go, A (2014) *Twitter Sentiment Classification Using Distant Supervision*. Available online at: http://s3.amazonaws.com/academia.edu.documents/34632156/Twitter_Sentiment_Classification_using_Distant_Supervision.pdf?AWSAccessKeyId=AKIAIWOWYYGZ2Y53UL3A&Expires=1485181578&Signature=BtYPKr0zgeE%2BYImw7UfadvLBIqI%3D&response-content-disposition=inline%3B%20filename%3DTwitter_Sentiment_Classification_using_D.pdf [accessed 23 January 2017].

Kaschub, M, Smith, J (2014) *Promising Practices in 21st Century Music Teacher Education*. Oxford: Oxford University Press, pp2–5.

Kirkwood, A, Price, L (2014) Technology-enhanced learning and teaching in higher education: what is 'enhanced' and how do we know? A critical literature review. *Learning, Media and Technology*, 39(1): 6–36.

Siemens, G (2005) *A Learning Theory for the Digital Age*. Available online at: http://devrijeruimte.org/content/artikelen/Connectivism.pdf [accessed 27 October 2016].

Tomlinson, C, Moon, T (2013) *Assessment and Student Success in a Differentiated Classroom*. Alexandria, VA: ASCD.

33
G Suite for education

What is G Suite?

As the technology giants make further inroads into education, it seems natural that Google should take much of the functionality of Google Drive and create a suite of educational products. At the time of writing, G Suite is free to education but not to business.

Though Google may want to lock in consumers by ensuring that G Suite works best with Google Chromebooks, they do see their role as enhancing, rather than replacing existing educational practices.

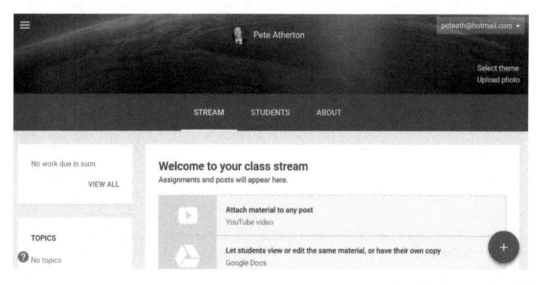

Image 33.1 The seductive ease of Google?

What can G Suite do for teachers and learners?

Google produced a highly informative presentation (on Google Slides, naturally) on G Suite in 2016. The presentation can be found here: **Goo.gl/d7Vqio** but parts of it are discussed below.

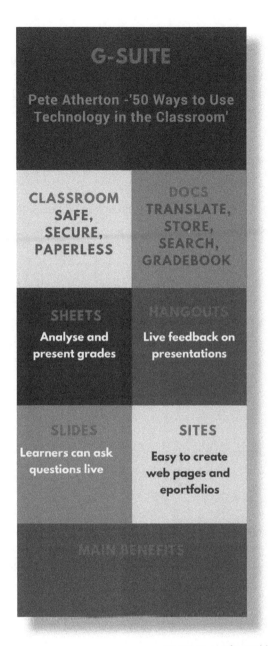

Image 33.2 Infographic: benefits of using G Suite

For teachers

Creating a paperless learning environment

Teachers can add their students to a class and form a safe, secure hub for news, assignments and feedback. Each assignment can incorporate Google Docs, videos, links and files from the teacher's computer.

Docs

Here's a secret: this book was written in the cloud. Each chapter was stored in Google Docs. I did this because I thought that, if the book is going to be data-heavy, it would be preferable to let Google take the strain, instead of my ageing MacBook. Like any teacher, though, I started getting excited about how Google Docs was making my life easier. Here is a short summary of some of the ways in which teachers may be seduced by Docs.

- Translate any document for English as an additional language learners.

- Share a parents' evening appointment sheet.

- Use an addon called 'Draftback' to track the progress and check the authenticity of the work created by a learner or group.

Sheets

Google Sheets essentially comprise the interface of Excel but with added features. As with Docs, the 'Explore' button adds value by tempting users to use tools to analyse their data. Hundreds of addons can improve the appearance or user experience or even facilitate deeper analysis of data.

Teachers can create an online gradebook via the Gradebook addon; this will show graphs of grade distribution and average scores. You can even use 'conditional formatting' to colour-code grades.

For learners

Docs

Students can learn collaboratively by being given access to the same document. This Google Doc can then be used for both teachers and learners to provide real-time feedback.

Slides

Learners are able to ask questions whilst viewing a presentation. All they have to do is 'join' the presentation via the link at the top of each slide. Other learners have the option to 'rate' each question with a 'thumbs up' or 'thumbs down'. Questions can be anonymised but that must be at the teacher's discretion.

Sites

A Google Site can be a website or an eportfolio. Learners should be enamoured with the ease with which they can create visually appealing web pages or organise all of their work into subjects and topics in a manageable eportfolio.

How to use G Suite

The entry-level way to start using many of G Suite's functions is to sign in to Google. This will provide access to Google Drive, which means that you can use Google Slides, Docs, Sites, Sheets and Forms. G Suite offers significant support in their website regarding how to get started.

📄 E-Portfolios

Students can keep records of their best work using sites as a E-Portfolio. They can organise their work by subject and can include as many pages as they require.

Students can also use Sites to write a blog or submit a project. You can also make a school template for your student's portfolios.

Image 33.3 Who needs paper? Google's eportfolio

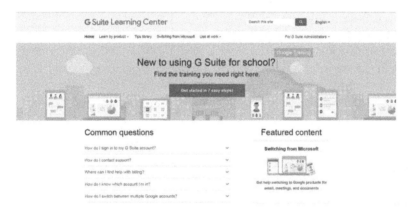

Image 33.4 Life is suite – extensive support for teachers

Research and reference without leaving Google Docs

Google Docs has an 'explore' button at the bottom right of the screen. This creates a sidebar, from which users can search without having to open a new window.

Cite sources

Turnitin is currently shifting its emphasis from enabling teachers to identify plagiarism to empowering learners to cite their sources correctly. G Suite's way of empowering learners to cite correctly can be located by using the 'Explore' button to use the search function as normal, then roll over the results to reveal an inverted commas icon. Clicking this will automatically cite the reference in the format that you requested.

G Suite for assessment

- Google Forms are an easy way to gather feedback from learners or parents. The 'charts' function will translate into an attractive chart.

- For rigorous peer assessment, Google Hangouts can allow learners to give live feedback to presentations, videos, experiments and so on.

- Google Docs: clicking on the + icon, then entering a user's email address allows peer assessment of the content of Google Docs. The teacher can create a feedback loop in this way. If you want more gentle formative assessment, the 'editing' drop-down menu (top right) can reveal the 'suggesting' function, in which all comments are classed as suggestions and are assigned to the person who made them.

G Suite for learning

Google's presence in the edtech landscape is bolstered by a reputation for ease of use and a slick brand personality. This brand image is given more gravitas by commissioning corporate research. An example of this is Watson and Pape's (2016) study into the impact of Google for education in four US districts. All studies revealed around a 20% improvement in graduation or achievement rates as a result of adopting Chromebooks and/or G Suite. Does this really reveal a genuine positive benefit or is it merely an example of the 'Gafa' companies (Google, Apple, Facebook and Amazon) exerting unchecked and potentially pernicious corporate power (Moore, 2017)? Critiques of the power and ethics of major corporations are, of course, commonplace but there is no space to explore them here.

Links to the Teachers' Standards

S1: Set high expectations which inspire, motivate and challenge pupils

The openness and transparency encouraged by G Suite can motivate pupils to stretch and challenge. The importance of maintaining security and appropriate behaviour conduct towards each other's work can help establish a safe environment.

S2: Promote good progress and outcomes by pupils

The 'starters and plenaries' function on Google Forms is designed to build on prior knowledge and address misconceptions.

S5: Adapt to the strengths and needs of all pupils

Not only does the interactive nature of Google Slides empower learners to ask questions, the sheer variety and ease of G Suite and its add ons are likely to offer appropriate support (if handled correctly).

S6: Make accurate and productive use of assessment

The fact that peers and teachers can edit documents helps create a formative dialogue.

References

Moore, M (2017) Society will be defined by how we deal with tech giants. *The Guardian*, pp1–2. Available online at: https://www.theguardian.com/commentisfree/2017/apr/01/brexit-britain-respond-tech-giants-civic-role-google-apple-facebook-amazon-eu [accessed 29 June 2017].

Watson, J, Pape, L (2016) *Impact Portraits: Success Stories with Google for Education*. Google. Available online at: https://www.blog.google/topics/education/impact-portraits-success-stories-google-education/ [accessed 29 June 2017].

34
Lino

Image 34.1 Always running out of Post-it notes? Virtual sticky notes: Lino

What is Lino?

Lino is a sticky notes and photo-sharing website for PC and iOS or Android devices. Many of us will be more familiar with the term 'Post-it notes' and will have been seduced by their combination of minimalism, ease of use and garish charm. Indeed, many educators of all persuasions and contexts will have used these magical accessories in their lessons. This chapter will acknowledge the pedagogic benefits of actual sticky notes but also consider the ways in which teachers and learners could benefit from also using sites like Lino. At this point it would be apt to reiterate that this book advocates using these edtech tools alongside, not instead of, analogue, physical resources.

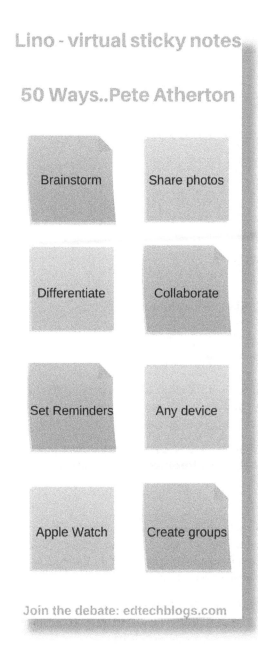

Image 34.2 Infographic: benefits of using Lino

What can Lino do for teachers and learners?

For teachers

The educational benefits of using Post-it notes are well documented across many blogs and articles and some of these are discussed during the literature review. Post-it notes help us create many teaching episodes for our lessons, some of which are summarised here:

- brainstorming;

- mind mapping;

- ranking;

- self-assessment;

- peer assessment;

- formative assessment by the teacher;

- bookmarking and annotation;

- storyboarding;

- flip books;

- classification/taxonomy;

- quick polls;

- plenaries (by sticking Post-its on a whiteboard);

- 'Who am I?' games;

- summarising learning.

It is fair to say that Lino offers all of the above and much more. Teachers could use Lino to set themselves sticky note reminders and share stickies with photos and videos for more interesting lessons. In many ways, Lino could be seen as a more convenient but less sophisticated version of Padlet.

The premium option is £3 a month and offers additional storage and improved search. Details of the premium option are here: **http://en.linoit.com/en/premium/**.

For learners

Lino's chief function is to enable the posting of virtual sticky notes. Another useful feature is the ability to colour-code content. This can help clarify and categorise information. It can also provide a way of differentiating without dumbing down content for lower achievers or offering exclusive tasks for the brighter learners. Like many edtech tools, users can work collaboratively and in real time.

Learners may be seduced by convenient features, some of which have been recently added.

- With Lino, contributions from the class can be saved, enhanced and shared.

- Lino is accessible via an Apple watch app. The app can be used to alert users when someone posts a sticky on their canvas. It can also help organise appointments, which can be peeled off when they have been completed.

- Lino can be used to share photos and videos related to school work. The appeal of this could be that these would not be seen and judged by learners' social media contacts.

- The interface feels bright and fun.

How to use Lino

The website boasts that Lino requires nothing but a web browser. Though a download is not essential, the app can be downloaded from the App Store for iOS devices and Google Play for Android.

Add stickies

Firstly, visit the homepage and select 'Give it a shot'. You can then experiment with dragging stickies on to your canvas (though it actually resembles a corkboard).

Share

At the bottom of each sticky there is an option to send your note to a member of your group or via email.

Set reminders

The Windows gadget allows you set sticky note reminders and alarms on your desktop.

Create a group

Visit **http://linoit.com/home/newGroup**. You can then name your group, give it an icon and set the membership to open or by invitation only.

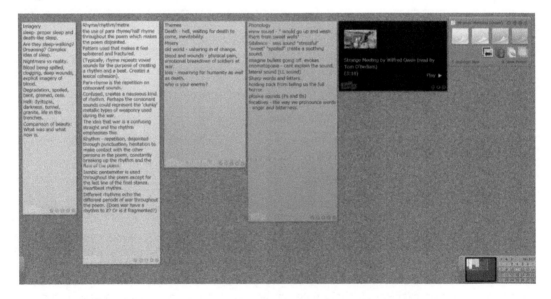

Image 34.3 Colour-coded analysis of war poetry with trainee English teachers

Lino for assessment

Virtual sticky notes

Assessing work with sticky notes is an efficient way to give swift but impactful feedback. The colours could be utilised to enable the teacher to walk around with a tablet and give verbal feedback but also add some comments to Lino. The colours could represent a group, a topic being worked on or headings (for example, 'themes', 'rhyme scheme' and 'imagery').

As illustrated above, you can plan differentiated questions using colour-coded virtual stickies. The questions above are, of course, based on Bloom's taxonomy.

Lino for learning

There are, of course, many other ways of creating virtual sticky notes or similar, for example, Popplet, Note.ly and Padlet. Another way to create a *de facto* virtual sticky note is by adding comments to ebooks, which can be an alternative to annotations in pencil (Cavanaugh, 2006).

Learning with sticky notes could be seen as constructivism at work. Constructivism is concerned with ways in which knowledge is constructed through social interactions (Vygotsky et al., 1978; McKinley, 2015) and this helps societies and experiences explain reality (Punch, 2014). One of the ways in which these interactions can be implemented is by learners engaging in role plays. They could create sticky notes in groups, then feed back on their peers' notes. In this way, this would engage learners in the roles of critical friend, tutor or summariser (Payne, 2009). Though this example of a social constructivist classroom relates to higher education, methods such as these lend themselves to the secondary and further education sectors.

Links to the Teachers' Standards

S1: Set high expectations which inspire, motivate and challenge pupils

Using learners as critical friends and tutors can be an effective way to stretch and challenge.

S2: Promote good progress and outcomes by pupils

Sticky notes help learners reflect on their learning goals and summarise their prior knowledge and the distance travelled in a lesson.

S4: Plan and teach well-structured lessons

The point above for S2 helps teachers top and tail a lesson.

S5: Adapt to the strengths and needs of all pupils

Colour-coded differentiated questions are easy to set up and recycle on Lino.

S6: Make accurate and productive use of assessment

Lino can be an improvement on sticky notes in the way that the notes can be saved, edited, enhanced with images and video, collaborated on and shared.

References

Cavanaugh, TW (2006) *Digital Reader: Using E-Books in K-12 Education.* Arlington, VA: International Society for Technology in Education.

McKinley, J (2015) Critical argument and writer identity: social constructivism as a theoretical framework for EFL academic writing. *Critical Inquiry in Language Studies,* 12(3): 184–207. doi:10.1080/15427 587.2015.1060558 [accessed 11 August 2017].

Payne, CR (2009) *Information Technology and Constructivism in Higher Education.* Hershey, PA: IGI Global.

Punch, K (2014) *Introduction to Research Methods in Education,* 2nd edition. London: SAGE.

Vygotsky, L, Cole, M, Stein, S, Sekula, A (1978) *Mind in Society.* Cambridge, MA: Harvard University Press.

35
Popplet

What is Popplet?

Popplet is a mind map tool, for PC, phone or tablet. It helps produce colour-coded mind maps and, as we will explore, graphic organisers.

The infographic in Image 35.1 is unique in this book, as its intention is to compare Popplet with MindMapfree, which is the subject of the next chapter.

What can Popplet do for teachers?

In the analogue days of education, brainstorming sessions and mind maps would be created with a great deal of effort on the part of the teacher, then lost forever. In many cases, mine included, the writing would be illegible.

For some tips on creating teaching activities either to stimulate interest in the content or to master it, search for Mike Gershon's The Ultimate Lesson Activity Generator, which summarises 120 teaching activities. One of many activities that could be completed using Popplet would be a 'silent debate', in which all participants in a group are assigned a colour and no talking is allowed. Learners are then asked to make connections between and annotate ideas.

How to use Popplet

The Popplet app can be downloaded from the App Store but you can also use Popplet via the website. To make a Popple – that is, to generate a mind map – you simply follow the on-screen instructions. The short tutorial takes you through how to add text and change the colour and size of the text or entire Popple. It also summarises how to create drawings or add images or videos.

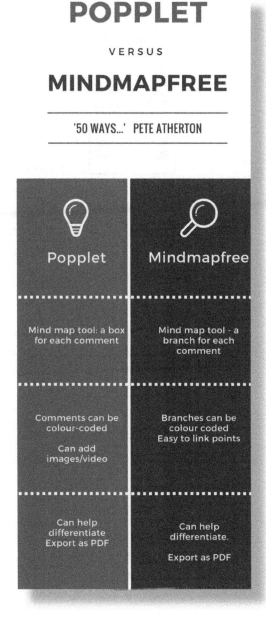

Image 35.1 Infographic: benefits of using Popplet and MindMapfree

It could be useful to know that Flash Player is required for Popplet to work. Though groups would need to sign up and use the same login, individuals could make a Popple without an account and simply print screen it.

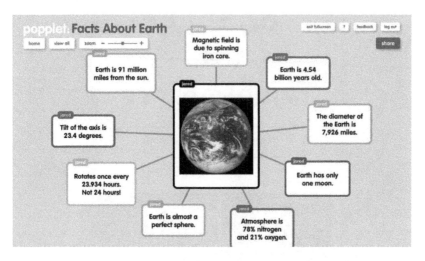

Image 35.2 Popplet: permanent mind maps

Popplet for assessment

Do you remember when creating mind maps, 'brainstorming' sessions or spider diagrams was a teacher-centred activity in which learners answered questions – directed or otherwise – and the teacher wrote the answers on the board? Where some sections of the class were passive and disengaged or were dutifully making notes that they did not understand?

Since those dark, analogue days, many ways of capturing, presenting and sharing learners' ideas have developed. For example, the teacher taking a photo of learners' mind maps, then sharing them on the same Google Slides presentation or Padlet wall can be an efficient way of giving learning some permanence. It can also show evidence of the trajectory of the learning.

Differentiation

The fact that it is easy to change the colour of text means that there are opportunities to show evidence of differentiation. Without being crude or obvious, the teacher could group learners according to ability and needs and/or performance. Though Popplet can be used for collaborative learning, it may be advisable to restrict this to small groups, as a whole-class Popplet could descend into chaos.

Popplet for learning

There are many theories about the benefits of mind mapping but this book will try and resist conflating psychology with educational theory.

Concept mapping

A concept map is a form of graphic organiser (Petty, 2014) that deconstructs the components of an idea. Where concept maps differ from mind maps is in their arrangement of information in boxes, ordered in logical and hierarchical progressions from top to bottom.

One such example of a concept map is the Frayer model (Teacher Tookit, 2017). In the Frayer model, the concept is in the centre of the page. There are four sections around it that help build relevant vocabulary: these sections are 'my definition', 'characteristics and facts', 'examples' and 'non-examples'. You can learn more about this on Teachertoolkit: **http://www.theteachertoolkit.com/index. php/tool/frayer-model**. Popplet, rather than MindMapfree, would help give more of a focus and structure to your online mind map.

Brainstorming

It is no surprise that Popplet is targeted at both education and business.

The theories behind business, carefully selected business practices, even personnel from the business sector are frequently appropriated by the world of education. This may be puzzling, even pernicious at times, but there are ways in which business-style brainstorming could provide some useful glimpses into the world of work.

Links to the Teachers' Standards

S1: Set high expectations which inspire, motivate and challenge pupils

The permanence of the mind maps, attribution of comments to names and novelty are likely to inspire and motivate.

S2: Promote good progress and outcomes by pupils

These tools are efficient ways to build on prior knowledge and structure guidance.

S4: Plan and teach well-structured lessons

The novelty and variety of Popplet help improve the structure of lessons.

S5: Adapt to the strengths and needs of all pupils

Mind maps and graphic organisers can be used to answer low- and high-order questions.

S6: Make accurate and productive use of assessment

They can also be used on tablets as revision aids or assignment plans. Feedback can be clear and the mind maps are easy to edit.

S8: Fulfil wider professional responsibilities

Mind maps can be shared at continuing professional development sessions on sharing good practice or edtech in the classroom.

References

Petty, G (2014) *Teaching Today: A Practical Guide,* 4th edition. Oxford: Oxford University Press.

Teachertoolkit (2017) Frayer model: the teacher toolkit. *Theteachertoolkit.com* [accessed 17 August 2017].

36
MindMapfree

What is MindMapfree?

Like Popplet, MindMapfree is an online mind map tool. Where MindMapfree differs from Popplet is in its potential to help construct more meandering mind maps and brainstorms. Popplet's boxes are more appropriate for structured mind maps or graphic organisers.

Before summarising this tool, it is worth noting that Canva and PowerPoint both have a mind map template. Also, there are several paid options on the market – for example, iMindmap – but this book aims to prioritise free tools. MindMapfree made it into *50 Ways to Use Technology Enhanced Learning in the Classroom* because it is a mindmap tool that is extremely easy to use and there is no need to download an app or any software.

The infographic for MindMapfree is in the previous chapter, as it is used to compare Popplet and Mindmapfree.

What can MindMapfree do for teachers and learners?

For teachers

MindMapfree is very easy to use and, like Popplet, provides strong evidence of learning having taken place. You can save your mind maps as an image file and the mind maps are flexible enough to build meandering, amorphous brainstorming or revision sessions. MindMapfree for learning will pick apart some of the contextual ideas surrounding mind mapping and brainstorming.

For learners

If you are a student, you can clearly see your contributions to the class. You may have the chance to get up in front of the class and add your point on the board. The more involved you are, the better chance you will have of remembering the content of the lesson and mastering the concepts.

How to use MindMapfree

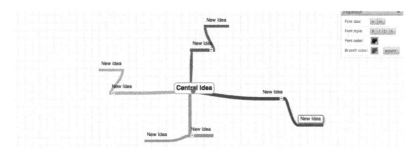

Image 36.1

Simply drag the red button at the centre (where it says, 'central idea') and type your idea or point. You can then roll over each new idea to locate another red button, which you drag to create linked points.

MindMapfree for assessment

The key here is making sure that you export your mind map as an image, so you can measure learners' progress from the first mind map to the second. As with Popplet, assigning a colour to learners means that they have a greater sense of accountability for their contributions.

Learners can be assessed on revision, understanding of terminology, number of key terms, strength of arguments, rationale, logic or creativity.

MindMapfree for learning

Why should a teacher consider using online mind maps? What is wrong with paper and card? The answer lies in the notion that, in the visually cluttered digital age, learners' intrinsic motivation can be improved by using colourful tools like MindMapfree. The reason for this is the way that intrinsic motivation is stimulated by novelty, agency and difficulty (Starkey, 2012). If that is true then teachers may need to continue to vary their edtech to maintain that novelty.

The notion of agency (Starkey, 2012) is similar to Deci and Ryan's idea of linking motivation to control (Deci and Ryan, 2008, cited in Dron and Anderson, 2015). Teachers would need to balance the need for challenge (Starkey, 2012) with the need to be within learners' range of competence (Deci and Ryan, 2008, cited in Dron and Anderson, 2015).

Links to the Teachers' Standards

Please refer to comments on Popplet (Chapter 35).

References

Dron, J, Anderson, T (2015) *Teaching Crowds: Learning and Social Media*. Edmonton, AB: AU Press.

Starkey, L (2012) *Teaching and Learning in the Digital Age*. London: Routledge.

37
WordPress

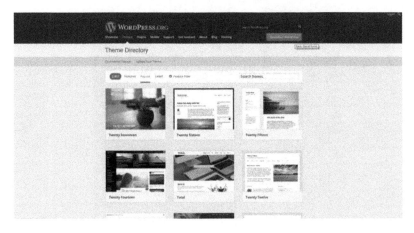

Image 37.1 WordPress.org - not to be confused with WordPress.com

What is WordPress?

WordPress is an open-source blogging and website-building platform, which removes the need for coding. It offers a relatively user-friendly and highly customisable way of facilitating and showcasing student work.

In addition to the potential for assessed activities, teachers may wish to explore the idea of developing their own personal, subject-specific or departmental website. With the right hosting options and connectivity, WordPress can be a sophisticated platform for high-profile websites. If not, it can help you produce a blog.

What can WordPress do for teachers and learners?

For teachers

A little preliminary work is necessary if your blog is going to be successful. For example, if you Google 'History teachers Twitter', you will discover resources, networking opportunities, free continuing

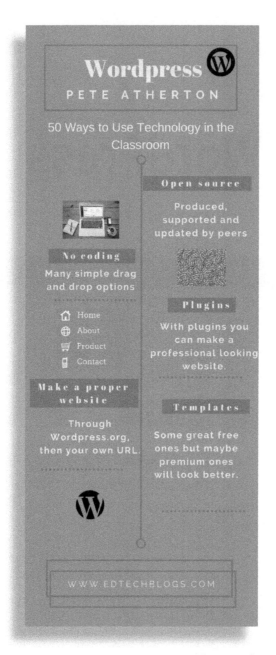

Image 37.2 Infographic: benefits of WordPress

professional development and stimulating debates. You can also find Twitter profiles with active, relevant blogs, such as @RusselTarr's blog, 'Tarr's Toolbox'. You can embed the tweets on your blog (open the tweet; click the drop-down menu; select 'embed tweet'; paste the code on to your blog) or simply curate a selection of tweets and blogs on your own blog.

Table 37.1 should give you some ideas on how to manage your expectations.

Table 37.1 *A differentiated guide to blogging as a teacher and learners*

	Teachers	Learners
Good	Post a monthly blog, with images	Post a blog as part of a specific piece of work. Master the skills required
Better	Post your take on other people's content (but no copying and pasting text). Lots of video, images. Share on virtual learning environment, email to staff and students	Post a weekly diary and commentary of findings relating to your subject
Best	Develop your own style and opinions on issues. Integrated with Twitter, a separate Facebook page, Instagram and LinkedIn	Share your blog with peers and staff. Present to the class; inspire others. Build a professional social media presence alongside your blog that is separate from your personal profiles
Off the scale	Add contributors, create engagement; make it shareable. Be an expert or opinion leader; use analytics (e.g. Google Analytics). Outsource logos and design to Fiverr or similar. Be an example to the rest of the staff	Make your blog something that would help you design websites on WordPress for payment

For learners

Though the table above should help, it is still important to plan your strategy before you ask learners to blog: set ground rules and take some time to answer all their questions; for example, 'How do I upload?', 'What will I write?', 'Will it be secure?' and 'How will I be assessed?' You will need to work closely with your IT department in advance of the launch of the blog, to ensure safety, responsibility and compliance.

How to use WordPress

WordPress as a blogging tool: WordPress.com

The more entry-level WordPress site is essentially a self-hosted blog. To do this, visit WordPress.com; select the layout, name, theme and plan. There are premium options but it may be more sensible to select free if it is your first blog.

WordPress.org

It may be judicious at this point to discriminate between WordPress.org and WordPress.com. WordPress.org offers the option of downloading the open-source WordPress software. Once this has been downloaded, you are free to make your own website. There are, of course, several obstacles in the way. Firstly, you will have already purchased a domain name from someone like Godaddy. You will need to purchase a hosting package from a hosting provider, for example, Hostgator. Once your new website has been created, you will need to select a theme.

Whether you are using WordPress.org or WordPress.com, the dashboard is very similar.

Perhaps the quickest ways of mastering the WordPress dashboard are through viewing instructional videos on YouTube and, when you encounter insurmountable technical issues, outsourcing small jobs to Fiverr.com. Remember, students learn more when their teachers can focus more on the content than the technology.

When you feel more confident, however, experiment with different templates and download some plugins. If you select 'plugins', then 'add plugins', you can tailor your search to match your needs. Try searching for 'best WordPress plugins' on Google and restrict your search to the last year.

WordPress for assessment

Collaborative writing

Your blog could be an immersive way to develop literacy. If you add learners as contributors (which may require the addition of a membership plugin like Buddypress), they have autonomy over the time and place of their contributions. You can then encourage collaboration on many activities. Here are some examples:

- creative writing;

- problem solving for science or maths;

- art/photography online exhibitions or festivals;

- showcasing and curation of creative work;

- travelogues for geography;

- demonstrations for PE or dance.

WordPress for learning

Web 1.0 versus Web 2.0

The mid-noughties marked the transition from the first incarnation of the internet, known as Web 1.0, to Web 2.0. Web 2.0 was decentralised: knowledge was democratised by websites like Wikipedia and other wikis, or websites that users can edit. Furthermore, the arrangement of information was seen as less of a taxonomy of topics and subjects, and more of a loose, interconnected web of tags (O'Reilly, 2009, p5). Crucially, Web 2.0 meant that teachers and children could make their own websites on platforms like WordPress.

This brave new internet world meant that teachers were no longer expected to be a 'sage on the stage', employed to deliver a one-way message, but a 'guide on the side', able to offer instant, powerful feedback (Noor Al Deen and Hendricks, 2013; Morrison, 2014).

WordPress is a potent legacy of Web 2.0, as the emphasis moves away from the teacher delivering knowledge towards learners actively demonstrating and disseminating their understanding. In doing so, learners are preparing themselves for the new economy (Cuban, 2001).

Links to the Teachers' Standards

S1: Set high expectations which inspire, motivate and challenge pupils

The beauty of blogging for stretch and challenge is giving learners the space to find their voice, develop their craft and have regular feedback.

S2: Promote good progress and outcomes by pupils

The space that blogs allow also helps learners reflect on their progress and emerging needs.

S3 Demonstrate good subject and curriculum knowledge

The teacher's blog can be a powerful way to showcase your expertise.

S4: Plan and teach well-structured lessons

The blog can be a regular reference point, with learners presenting, supporting and sharing good practice.

S5: Adapt to the strengths and needs of all pupils

The openness of a blog helps remove the glass ceiling for all learners and their learning styles.

S6: Make accurate and productive use of assessment

There are many ways to peer assess, self-assess and create a feedback loop through a blog.

The success criteria would be readily available to learners.

S8: Fulfil wider professional responsibilities

Your blog or your learners' blog could gain national - even international - recognition.

References

Noor Al Deen, H, Hendricks, J (2013) *Social Media and Strategic Communications*. Basingstoke: Palgrave Macmillan.

Cuban, L (2001) *Oversold and Underused*. Cambridge, MA: Harvard University Press.

Education Endowment Foundation (2016) *A Marked Improvement? A Review of the Evidence of Written Marking*. Oxford: University of Oxford. Available online at: https://educationendowmentfounda tion.org.uk/public/files/Publications/EEF_Marking_Review_April_2016.pdf [accessed 14 August 2017].

Morrison, CD (2014) From 'sage on the stage' to 'guide on the side': a good start. *International Journal for the Scholarship of Teaching and Learning*, 8: 1.

O'Reilly, T (2009) What is web 2.0? Design patterns and business models for the next generation of software. *O'Reilly*. Web. 14 August 2017.

38
Notability

What is Notability?

Notability is a neat notetaking app for tablet and smartphone. At the time of writing, Notability could be viewed on Gingerlabs.com; searching for either Gingerlabs or Notability will get you to the same destination. It can be downloaded to iOS devices from the iTunes Store.

What can Notability do for teachers and learners?

For teachers

It is easy to create very helpful multimedia resources using Notability. On the same 'note', you can add typed text, sketch drawings and add images and audio. These are easy to edit by tapping the highlight, erase or cut icons. The options for saving your 'notes' are helpfully diverse; for example, you can save your work in cloud-based services like Google Drive, iCloud and Dropbox.

Once you have completed your spontaneous ideas or detailed resources, you can password-protect specific files. This could be useful if you are asking learners to collaborate through your login.

For learners

Revision notes

For many learners, the cognitive processes needed for learning to take place often involve making connections between facts, ideas and concepts in a way that suits often diverse learning styles. Below is an example of how to do this through Notability.

Using Notability to revise GCSE biology

- Type a summary of evolution in a similar way to bullet points or a mind map
- Use the pencil tool to make connections between a list of concepts
- Take a PDF of a past paper or revision notes and annotate it

Import a web page (an instructional video, a diagram, for example)

- Create their own diagrams to aid or show understanding
- Add an audio commentary to clarify the notes
- Create a note purely to go through the mental and practical process of trying to answer a question

Image 38.1 Infographic: benefits of using Notability

How to use Notability

To set up Notability for frequent notetaking, consider playing with the settings. You can set the mode to light or dark, create your default background and also determine whether or not your sketches will be in colour. Notes can also be colour-coded to help you organise your resources. Left-handed people can even be accommodated by setting the hand-writing function to left-handed.

Tapping the + icon (top right) enables you to add or take photos and add web pages, virtual sticky notes or figures. In the same way that you would edit any other content on Notability, these additions can be cropped through the edit menu, moved by dragging or resized by pinching. Applying two fingers to a photo offers the ability to edit, copy or delete.

If you want to import a web page, you locate it, then tap 'done'. This will then add the page to your note; you can, of course, move, resize, crop, annotate or add a caption to the web page.

Notability for assessment

Assessed notetaking

The teacher could conduct frequent checks on learners' notetaking against some agreed success criteria. Some suggestions for what these criteria could look like might be:

- evidence of thinking;

- summarising and justifying any web pages;

- giving any web pages a reliability score out of ten;

- clarity of content;

- making clear connections.

You could, of course, tailor these to the exam grading criteria. In terms of differentiation, you would want every learner to be able to demonstrate success but be rewarded for stretch and challenge.

Edit images, photos, PDFs, web pages

Working alone or in small groups, your learners could be given work based on a piece of stimulus material. This could be a diagnostic test, a brainstorming session, an assessment of prior knowledge, even a summative task.

Micro teaches

Notability can be an innovative way for students to demonstrate their learning, for their peers to provide feedback and for the class to have access to content after each lesson.

Notability for learning

Divergent thinking

A way for Notability to help with divergent thinking would be to use it in a similar way to a Lotus Blossom exercise. Learners could create a sprawling, unfocused note, then be asked to create a new note for each topic or idea (Fisher and Frey, 2014). This could help learners embrace the discovery of problems to be solved (Starko, 2010) and equip them with the skills of divergent thinking that are necessary for the digital age (Wheadon, 2017). These uses of the two tools would also be effective examples of how graphic organisers and self-assessment can have a clear effect on learner progress (Petty, 2014).

Links to the Teachers' Standards

S1: Set high expectations which inspire, motivate and challenge pupils

Stretch and challenge: more immersive and thoughtful notes can open up many possibilities to examine learners' metacognition.

S2: Promote good progress and outcomes by pupils

One of the ways that learners' progress is assessed is through 'work scrutinies'. You can use Notability as a fast way to demonstrate learning.

S3: Demonstrate good subject and curriculum knowledge

The teacher can store and share spontaneous notes from lessons or additional reading. These can be used to show that you are updating your subject knowledge.

S4: Plan and teach well-structured lessons

As with many edtech platforms, Notability could form a regular feature of your lessons, perhaps as a starter or a plenary to each lesson. Alternatively, you could roll out Notability on a particular day of the week, so the learners anticipate it.

S5: Adapt to the strengths and needs of all pupils

The many suggestions for how learners could use Notability will help you show that you are providing individualised support.

S6: Make accurate and productive use of assessment

The collaborative function of Notability provides significant scope for peer assessment and on-the-fly support to address misconceptions.

S8: Fulfil wider professional responsibilities

If you have a particularly impressive learner, his or her notes could be displayed on social media and on electronic display boards around the school.

References

Fisher, D, Frey, N (2014) *Checking for Understanding.* Alexandria, VA: ASCD.

Petty, G (2014) *Teaching Today: A Practical Guide,* 4th edition. Oxford: Oxford University Press.

Starko, A (2010) *Creativity in the Classroom.* New York: Routledge.

Wheadon, C (2017) Measuring progress towards GCSE English. *The No More Marking Blog.* Available online at: https://blog.nomoremarking.com/measuring-progress-towards-gcse-english-8ed4006c025e [accessed 5 July 2017].

Games, polls and student response systems

39
Slido

What is Slido?

Slido is an online polling tool or audience response system. It facilitates interaction at conferences but also has clear uses in a classroom. Participants join a poll by entering a code in the box on the homepage.

Teachers (or presenters) can try Slido free and have three polls per event, interactive questions and answers (Q&A), Twitter integration and an infographic of the responses.

What can Slido do for teachers and learners?

For teachers

Instant feedback is, unsurprisingly, a recurrent theme in this book. If learners are engaged in activity, they could be asked to break off from the task and ask a question. This question could be out of curiosity or for clarification. You may want to draw up a careful contract before doing this, maybe agreeing that questions are only allowed during the allocated time for using Slido. Learners could be encouraged to write down their questions so they are less likely to forget them. This could reduce the ever-present risk of edtech de-skilling students' literacy.

In terms of behaviour management, teachers could deploy a teaching assistant to moderate the polls if any comments or votes become inappropriate or unhelpful. This moderation role could also be delegated to a pair of trusted learners, perhaps in rotation. In addition to improving classroom management by asking learners to think carefully about their questions before asking them, an anonymous Q&A could help develop learners' high-order thinking skills. If learners are to ask questions via a poll, they will need to have thought more carefully about them than if they simply shout them out. The teacher could consider hiding the board from the class until the questions have been moderated. That way, disruptive or malicious questions could be extinguished at source.

For learners

Slides

Teachers could simply share using the 'slides' feature on Slido. That way, the slides would be accessible and in the pocket of every learner.

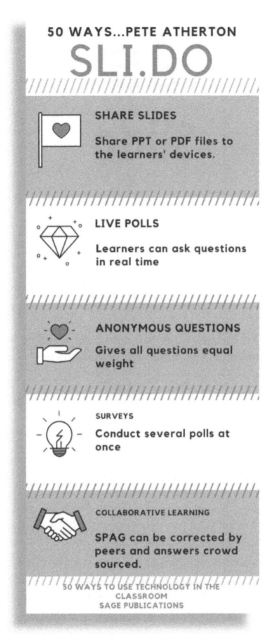

50 WAYS...PETE ATHERTON

SLI.DO

SHARE SLIDES

Share PPT or PDF files to the learners' devices.

LIVE POLLS

Learners can ask questions in real time

ANONYMOUS QUESTIONS

Gives all questions equal weight

SURVEYS

Conduct several polls at once

COLLABORATIVE LEARNING

SPAG can be corrected by peers and answers crowd sourced.

50 WAYS TO USE TECHNOLOGY IN THE CLASSROOM
SAGE PUBLICATIONS

Image 39.1 Infographic: benefits of using Slido

Self-efficacy

Learners value being in control of their learning. At times, that desire for control can be frustrated, as they can rarely have much influence over the direction or content of a lesson. To address this, Slido can give more control to the learners; one of the testimonials on the website refers to the idea of giving power to questions. It can often be the case that only the loudest or most confident have their questions answered: anonymised polling can give space and gravitas to thoughts that would otherwise have been suppressed.

How to use Slido

Create questions

The presenter or teacher asks the audience or class to join by entering a code. They can then roll over the buttons to the right of each band and either promote a question to the top or delete it altogether. Participants can 'like' a question by clicking the 'thumbs up' icon. The more 'likes' a question receives, the higher it ranks and the more likely it is to be answered.

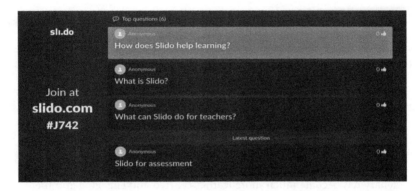

Image 39.2 How important is the popularity of a question?

Polls

To create a poll, first select 'poll type'. Several polls can be created at the same time, all of which can be accessed through entering a code on the homepage. Clicking 'edit' enables you to create a survey, which will produce more in-depth data.

Events

An 'event' is a Q&A that allows the audience at one of your presentations to ask questions. Polls can be open text questions, multiple choice or a simple star rating. At this point, comparisons could be made with Ping Pong (not in this edition) – on which the audience can respond with emojis and drawings – and Twitter polls, where the progress of responses is also instantly displayed.

Slido for assessment

Slido (and other polling apps) can be valuable additions to a teacher's formative assessment toolkit. Consider using Slido for the following methods of assessing learners.

- The class ask questions in small groups as part of a Socratic seminar (where questions are answered with questions).

- In a 'no hands up' activity, Slido is used as a way of giving an answer and gauging how many answered correctly. In pairs, learners could enquire about the reasons for each answer and this could be recorded on paper.

- Student presentations could have live polls to ensure that all are still active and engaged.

Slido for learning

Infographics

Slido produces infographics from responses to questions. These can, like word clouds on Poll Everywhere, open up lines of enquiry and develop high-order thinking (Barrass, 2005). Frequent occurrence should not be confused with significance but stimulating debate has to be welcomed (Atherton, 2017).

SAMR model: substitution, augmentation, modification, redefinition

To update Puentedura's (2006) model (cited in Walsh, 2015), online polls start by substituting hands up for voting with handsets. This can augment the learning experience by crowdsourcing answers or displaying and analysing results. Modification of a task effectively redesigns it: in this case a simple plenary has become much more learner-centred and engaging and there is visual evidence of learning taking place. To an extent, Petty's (2014) notion of 'assertive questioning' can be practised through live polling, as can deeper probing from the teacher or peer evaluation of questions (Capel et al., 2016).

At the redefinition stage (Puentedura, 2006, cited in Walsh, 2015), tasks that were previously impossible become a regular part of the lesson. An example of this is Slido's 'slides' feature, which can push a presentation on PowerPoint or PDF to each learner's phone. Here, the presentation should contain carefully constructed questions for the learners to answer.

Links to the Teachers' Standards

S1: Set high expectations which inspire, motivate and challenge pupils

Use of teaching assistant or trusted learner can complement a learner-generated contract about acceptable conduct. Requesting that learners ask each other why they answered how they did, live interaction during activities and crowdsourcing answers can all help stretch and challenge. In a poll, there is no 'wrong' answer – just a chance to share answers and deconstruct the reasons for them.

S3: Demonstrate good subject and curriculum knowledge

Addressing misunderstandings can be achieved in a more democratic way. Spelling and grammar errors can be corrected anonymously by peers. Scholarship can be encouraged by sharing interactive slides, then polling about those.

S4: Plan and teach well-structured lessons

Slido can help create engaging learning episodes and slides can encourage flipped learning.

S5: Adapt to the strengths and needs of all pupils

A great deal of the differentiation will depend on the groupings and choice of questions.

S6: Make accurate and productive use of assessment

Slido is highly effective for showing evidence of formative assessment and mapping a learning journey.

S8: Fulfil wider professional responsibilities

Deployment of a teaching assistant, polling parents and stakeholders and easy sharing content on social media can help contribute to the wider ethos of the institution.

References

Atherton, P (2017) *Kahoot for Assessment*. Liverpool: Kindle. Available online at: https://www.amazon.co.uk/Using-Kahoot-Assessment-teachers-learners-ebook/dp/B071CJSTC4/ref=sr_1_1?ie=UTF8&qid=1492696884&sr=8-1&keywords=pete+atherton [accessed 11 July 2017].

Barrass, R (2005) *Students Must Write: A Guide to Better Writing in Coursework and Examinations (Routledge Study Guides)*, 3rd edition. London: Routledge.

Capel, S, Leask, M, Younie, S (2016) *Learning to Teach in the Secondary School,* 7th edition. London: Routledge.

Petty, G (2014) *Evidence-Based Teaching*. Oxford: Oxford University Press.

Walsh, K (2015) 8 examples of transforming lessons through the SAMR cycle. *Emerging Edtech*. Available online at: http://www.emergingedtech.com/2015/04/examples-of-transforming-lessons- [accessed 15 September 2017].

40
Kahoot!

What is Kahoot!?

Kahoot! is a game-based student response system (GSRS), which was launched in 2012. Kahoot! reached 40 million monthly users in 2017 (GetKahoot.com, 2017). It appears that ease of use has been one of the major factors in its popularity. It is frequently used by experienced and trainee teachers as a reward for their learners. Can it also be a powerful way to empower learners to reflect on *how* they learn and for teachers to demonstrate the extent of the learning?

What can Kahoot! do for teachers and learners?

For teachers

As the infographic indicates, Kahoot! offers significant scope for teachers to enhance their lessons. It is free and there is no need to make an account (though some of their funding is predicated on the generation of revenue from corporate clients). Users can make their own quizzes and there is already an extensive bank of quizzes from other Kahoot! users. Users can even join or launch a global quiz in real time.

For learners

Younger children, teenagers and adults all share a propensity to be energised and motivated by the competitive, gamified nature of Kahoot! Chapter 2 on gamified learning goes into more depth about the uses and context of gamification. The 'Kahoot! for learning' section of this chapter provides a review of some of the literature that is relevant to this and similar student response systems.

You may want to think carefully about how the dynamic of each class will influence their enjoyment of Kahoot! You may also want to use Kahoot! quizzes and discussions as a way to develop high-order thinking, paired work and your own questioning skills.

Image 40.1 Infographic: benefits of using Kahoot!

How to use Kahoot!

Once you have registered through Kahoot.com, you can create a new quiz. Learners would then fill in the boxes to give the quiz a title, description, visibility level and so on. When you have found or made your quiz, select 'launch quiz', then students join by entering a code. If you are daunted by

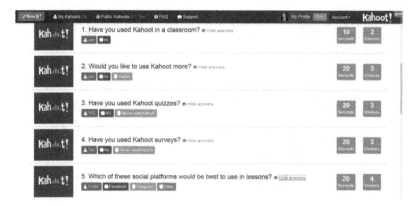

Image 40.2 Quick and easy questionnaires through Kahoot!

the thought of making your own, you can always discover thousands of quizzes or use the search box to find something more tailored to your own needs.

Kahoot! for assessment

This section will provide an example of how a 'Blind Kahoot!' can encourage teachers to think more carefully about the preparation of their questioning.

How a Blind Kahoot! can improve your questioning and help scaffold learning

- Use an introductory question to set the scene.

- Pose a challenging question, to which learners are not expected to know the answer.

- Create a question designed to help learners explain and discuss their answers.

- Make a reinforcement question to apply the new knowledge.

- Make several more reinforcement questions, using different examples.

- Ask the 'blind' question again, but this time learners will have a good chance of answering.

- Pose a new 'blind' question, perhaps to teach the exception to the rule.

- Ask a no-points question to help explain the previous answer.

- Ask several reinforcement questions.

- Ask the second 'blind' question again.

- Ask a 'compound reinforcement question' (Castle, 2017, cited in Atherton, 2017) to test everything learned so far.

- Repeat to help you meet the learning objectives.

- Play again in 'Ghost mode' to beat the previous score.

(Kahoot, 2017, cited in Atherton, 2017)

Kahoot! for learning

As a GSRS (Wang, 2014), Kahoot! can be viewed as performing essential functions of any gamified learning, most notably that of sustaining intrinsic motivation (Malone, 1980, cited in Wang, 2014). Examples of these are the way Kahoot!'s interface is designed to create a fantasy world, stimulate and sustain curiosity and present levels of challenge (Wang, 2014). Indeed, you may have noticed how much more engaged learners can be when learning feels like a game. This must, of course, be balanced against the need to prepare them for the real (and very much analogue) worlds of examinations and work.

Links to the Teachers' Standards

S1: Set high expectations which inspire, motivate and challenge pupils

If intrinsic motivation is high and sustained, this is more likely to inspire and challenge. The questioning and feedback, of course, will be crucial here.

S2: Promote good progress and outcomes by pupils

A 'Blind Kahoot', then playing again in ghost mode, provides an excellent way to build on prior knowledge.

S3: Demonstrate good subject and curriculum knowledge

The formative data can be a highly effective way to address misunderstandings. Scholarship can be promoted by asking learners to reveal the reasons for their answers and thinking to each other.

S4: Plan and teach well-structured lessons

Games can promote a love of learning, but be careful that you do not exclude certain learners from recognition and reward. The Kahoot! discussion can promote intellectual curiosity, perhaps through visual stimuli.

S5: Adapt to the strengths and needs of all pupils

The section on using a 'Blind Kahoot!' helps you provide evidence of how each learner reacted to specific levels and timings of questions.

S6: Make accurate and productive use of assessment

If the questions are thoughtfully designed and the data employed to frame effective feedback, Kahoot! can be a powerful formative assessment tool.

(Continued)

(Continued)

S7: Manage behaviour effectively to ensure a good and safe environment

Competitive quizzes can present behaviour management issues, so setting clear expectations is paramount here.

S8: Fulfil wider professional responsibilities

When both you and your learners thrive from using Kahoot! this can present opportunities for you to share good practice.

References

Atherton, P (2017) *Using Kahoot! for Assessment: What Kahoot! Can Do for Teachers and Learners.* Amazon. Available online at: http://amzn.to/2q7B3ry [accessed 7 August 2017].

GetKahoot.com (2017) Kahoot! | Learning Games | Make Learning Awesome! Available online at: http://getkahoot.com [accessed 1 October 2017].

Wang, A (2014) The wear out effect of a game-based student response system. *Computers & Education*, 82: 1–22. Available online at: http://www.sciencedirect.com/science/article/pii/S0360131514002516 [accessed 11 October 2016].

41
Quizlet

What is Quizlet?

At its most simple level, Quizlet is a website that makes use of virtual flashcards. Teachers can use these flashcards to quiz and test their learners; learners can use the flashcards to learn new topics or revise existing ones.

The Quizlet blog shares tips on how to use Quizlet in a variety of contexts. Some of these will be debated in the section on 'Quizlet for learning'. This chapter will be concerned with the free version but there is a premium package too. The paid option was £19.99 a year at the time of writing.

What can Quizlet do for teachers and learners?

For teachers

The ease with which teachers can build interactive and visually appealing quizzes is one of Quizlet's best qualities. Flashcards can be displayed with or without audio; there is also the flexibility to start with the definition, the term in question or both.

Similar to Kahoot!, Quizlet also offers collaborative classroom games, like Quizlet Live. Teachers can also use Quizlet to play bingo: if you search online for 'make your own bingo cards', you can print out the cards for each group, then select 'shuffle' mode in the flashcard feature.

For learners

Quizlet employs visual/spatial learning styles in a way that can encourage competition between groups or test learners' individual progress. It can also provide ipsative assessment (Atherton, 2017) to help motivate learners to surpass their personal best.

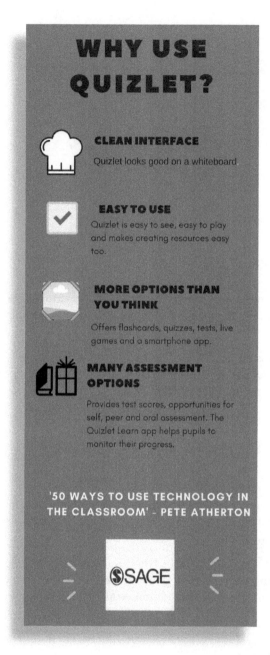

WHY USE QUIZLET?

CLEAN INTERFACE
Quizlet looks good on a whiteboard

EASY TO USE
Quizlet is easy to see, easy to play and makes creating resources easy too.

MORE OPTIONS THAN YOU THINK
Offers flashcards, quizzes, tests, live games and a smartphone app.

MANY ASSESSMENT OPTIONS
Provides test scores, opportunities for self, peer and oral assessment. The Quizlet Learn app helps pupils to monitor their progress.

'50 WAYS TO USE TECHNOLOGY IN THE CLASSROOM' - PETE ATHERTON

⑤SAGE

Image 41.1 Infographic: benefits of using Quizlet

How to use Quizlet

Register

Though the ways of integrating Quizlet into teaching and learning are discussed later, using the basic version is very straightforward. You register via email or through your Facebook or Google+

account. You may be asked to consider upgrading to the paid version but you can continue using Quizlet for free.

Create a class

The next step is to ask your students to join, which you can do by email. The learners will have to accept their emailed instructions if they want to join the class.

Quizlet Live

This option asks teachers to send their set of flashcards to 'Live'. This then sends learners to Quizlet. live, from where they join the game by entering the code.

Image 41.2

Like Kahoot!, they will be asked by the teacher to form teams, whose progress will be viewable to increase a sense of competition.

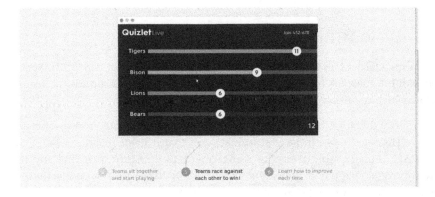

Image 41.3

Creating 'a new study set' is another way of asking you to create new flashcards. The term will be on one side, the definition on the other.

Quizlet for assessment

Quizlet make it clear on their website that they are a self-study tool, not an assessment tool. That said, you can monitor the performance of individuals and teams by using the 'class progress' feature. This will help teachers identify the areas of ease and struggle.

Spell

The spell feature asks learners to simply type what they hear. This may be particularly appropriate for modern foreign languages and English as an additional/foreign language learners.

Match

Useful as a starter, a plenary or revision activity, the 'match' function requires learners to drag images or words to match their definitions. You can add intensity to proceedings by making teams compete against the clock.

Learn – for self and individual assessment

This ambitious feature is 'powered' by Quizlet's Learning Assistant Platform, which claims to combine research into cognitive science with individual mastery needs. Quizlet Learn will ultimately create an adaptive study plan, which will monitor progress and reward achievement.

Test

This function offers four options: written, matching, multiple choice and true or false. Users create a new test, answer the questions and are then given a 'grade' in the form of a percentage.

Quizlet for learning

In many respects, Quizlet helps people learn in a behaviourist way (Skinner, 2011). Behaviourism is concerned with how people's behaviour can be conditioned. Quizlet flashcards can be used to learn by repetition, which can be an effective way to learn.

If applied correctly this substitution of physical flashcards for augmented virtual ones (Puentedura, 2015, cited in Hunter, 2015) can be transformative in that it helps redefine what a classroom is (Hunter, 2015). Similarly radical ways of using edtech to transform teaching and learning are referred to in several chapters in this book, most notably the notion of connectivism (Siemens, 2005) and the flipped classroom (Mazur, 2014; Scheg, 2015).

Links to the Teachers' Standards

S1: Set high expectations which inspire, motivate and challenge pupils

You can graduate the level of challenge through the questions on the flashcards and also set offline extension tasks, for example, mini-presentations, written responses to hypotheses or problems about related concepts.

S2: Promote good progress and outcomes by pupils

Used as a test or revision/review exercise, Quizlet can build confidence around prior knowledge and help address weaknesses.

S5: Adapt to the strengths and needs of all pupils

If you use data to help organise your groups, Quizlet Live can be conducted in carefully differentiated groups. The way you structure your questions can ensure that you have the required level of scaffolding and challenge.

S6: Make accurate and productive use of assessment

Flashcards offer many opportunities for addressing misconceptions, offering oral feedback and tracking achievement through empirical formative assessment.

S8: Fulfil wider professional responsibilities

Fun activities can easily become fun events that can be captured and shared on social media and communicated to colleagues and parents.

References

Atherton, P (2017) *Kahoot for Assessment*. Liverpool: Kindle. Available online at: https://www.amazon.co.uk/Using-Kahoot-Assessment-teachers-learners-ebook/dp/B071CJSTC4/ref=sr_1_1?ie=UTF8&qid=1492696884&sr=8-1&keywords=pete+atherton [accessed 20 April 2017].

Hunter, J (2015) *Technology Integration and High Possibility Classrooms*. New York: Routledge.

Mazur, E (2014) *Peer Instruction*. Harlow: Pearson Education.

Scheg, A (2015) *Implementation and Critical Assessment of the Flipped Classroom Experience*. Hershey, PA: Information Science Reference.

Siemens, G (2005) *A Learning Theory for the Digital Age*. Available online at: http://devrijeruimte.org/content/artikelen/Connectivism.pdf [accessed 27 October 2016].

Skinner, BF (2011) *About Behaviourism*. London: Vintage.

42

GoSoapBox

What is GoSoapBox?

There are a growing number of live feedback and assessment tools. In this crowded arena, GoSoapBox's unique selling points could be the 'confusion barometer' and the 'social Q&A' feature. Other features – though not unique – could be very welcome as part of the same package. Examples of these are GoSoapBox's live polling, quizzes, the option of joining by entering a code and open-ended feedback.

What can GoSoapBox do for teachers and learners?

For teachers

Some teachers may be drawn towards the convenience of having all these features under one roof:

- easy access for learners;
- quizzes;
- polls;
- discussions;
- ability to moderate with profanity filters;
- ability to add a moderator;
- instant and clear formative assessment data;
- a 'confusion barometer';
- 'social Q&A'.

You may want to think carefully about how much your learners value such varied edtech platforms and balance this against how well they learn through them.

Image 42.1 Infographic: benefits of using GoSoapBox

For learners

As with Kahoot!, Goformative, Classkick and many more, the learners will have the luxury of instant feedback. They may also be familiar with other clicker tools.

How to use GoSoapBox

Events: create a new event

Simply click 'create an event' – an event refers to any activity that you conduct with your class.

Joining an event

Click 'manage this GoSoapBox event' and this will generate a nine-digit event access code. The code will be displayed on the screen. The class join the 'event' by entering the code into **app.gosoap box.com**.

Moderation panel

This gives teachers the ability to activate or deactivate features such as the 'confusion barometer', quizzes, instant polling, social Q&A or the profanity filter.

GoSoapBox for assessment

Questions feature: high-order questions

In terms of in-class feedback, GoSoapBox's 'questions' feature could provide teachers with a mini-epiphany. The revelation is this: if high-order thinking skills are so important, why not reward learners for the quality of their questions?

A poster of Bloom's taxonomy could be a useful visual prompt to reinforce what high-order questions look like (Blooms Taxonomy Teacher Planning Kit, 2015). Table 42.1 gives some introductory ideas.

Table 42.1 Examples of low- and high-order questions

Low: Remembering	What or who is/how many/describe?
Low: Comprehension	Explain/compare/what is revealed?
Application	What examples could you give?
High: Analysis	What does this represent? Compare to similar examples
High: Synthesis	Can you invent? How would you adapt?
High: Evaluation	What information led you to this view and why?

Adapted from Bloom's Taxonomy Teacher Planning Kit (2015).

What rewards would you like to give to your learners for the self-awareness of their questions? How could you emphasise that low-order questions are not inferior but are actually important stepping stones to developing your thinking skills? When people begin a statement with high-order thinking, they can be difficult to understand. When they only express low-order thinking, they limit their thinking and, by implication, actions.

Checking understanding: the 'confusion barometer'

The 'confusion barometer' opens up opportunities for the teacher to check understanding. If, however, learners declare themselves as 'confused', you may want to think about what the next strategies would be in terms of scaffolding.

Quizzes

The quizzes provide colour-coded feedback on each quiz. If you display the results on the board but conceal the names, this will enable the class to drill down into the reasons for certain questions being too hard or too easy.

Polls

Polls reveal learners' responses as a pie graph. The information can be an efficient way to demonstrate the distance travelled in the lesson, from a diagnostic test to an exit ticket.

GoSoapBox for learning

In-class assessment

It may be worth considering the importance of planning questions to help equip students with the skills to gain the higher summative marks (Capel et al., 2009). One of the problems that GoSoapBox may solve is teachers asking too many questions on their feet, to the whole class. This absence of forethought results in a preponderance of low-order questions. By contrast, high-order thinking has been shown to increase both achievement and motivation (Brookhart, 2010).

Technology enhanced learning and feedback

A significant proportion of the literature is concerned with providing largely summative feedback to university students. University practices, though, do have an impact on schools and colleges; examples of these are Turnitin's inroads into schools and emerging assessment platforms like WISEflow and Myknowledgemap – which are not only device-agnostic but sector-agnostic too. These tools are also concerned with helping educators provide meaningful formative assessment and promote self-regulation (Nicol and Milligan, 2006).

If GoSoapBox can offer a transformative contribution to in-class formative assessment and help develop high-order thinking, it could be viewed in tandem with formative feedback on written work. In contrast to the need to develop critical, evaluative thinking, feedback can work best when it is descriptive, not evaluative (Wiggins, 2001, cited in Nicol and Milligan, 2006). In 2015, the University of Portsmouth piloted an app that enabled students to view all their feedback in the same place. How likely is it that learners will one day be able to access their in-class assessment and feedback and their summative grades from all of their subjects in one app?

Links to the Teachers' Standards

S1: Set high expectations which inspire, motivate and challenge pupils

The frequent opportunities to check understanding can beat a path to stretching and challenging the learners.

S2: Promote good progress and outcomes by pupils

The notion of a plenary can often present behaviour management issues. The 'social Q&A' could help focus learners and make them more accountable.

S3: Demonstrate good subject and curriculum knowledge

The 'social Q&A' can help you develop varied questioning techniques to help your subject knowledge.

S4: Plan and teach well-structured lessons

There are a variety of accessible and easy to use activities, for example polls, quizzes and discussions.

S5: Adapt to the strengths and needs of all pupils

The 'confusion barometer' could be mapped against baseline and other summative data and used to help differentiate.

S6: Make accurate and productive use of assessment

GoSoapBox generates formative assessment and engagement data.

S7: Manage behaviour effectively to ensure a good and safe environment

On one hand, the learners can be anonymous in their contributions. On the other, their names can be displayed and linked to formative data.

References

Bloom's Taxonomy Teacher Planning Kit (2015) Available online at: http://www.cebm.net/wp-content/uploads/2016/09/Blooms-Taxonomy-Teacher-Planning-Kit.pdf [accessed 16 August 2017].

Brookhart, S (2010) *How to Assess Higher-Order Thinking Skills in Your Classroom*. Alexandria, VA: ASCD.

Nicol, DJ, Milligan, C (2006) Rethinking technology-supported assessment in terms of the seven principles of good feedback practice. In Bryan, C, Clegg, K (eds.) *Innovative Assessment in Higher Education*. London: Taylor & Francis.

Capel, S, Leask, M, Turner, T (2009) *Learning to Teach in the Secondary School*. London: Routledge.

43
Poll Everywhere

What is Poll Everywhere?

Poll Everywhere is a classroom response system. Its uses in education range from identifying gaps in understanding and addressing misunderstandings to encouraging a more open forum for communication. The app enables you to embed polls in your presentations, through Google Slides, PowerPoint or Keynote.

For secondary schools (K-12 in the USA) there is a free version. There are some features that are premium only. At the time of writing, schools have to pay if they want to be able to display the correct answers, create sophisticated reports on results, and moderate and censor polls.

What can Poll Everywhere do for teachers and learners?

For teachers

Starter activities

Multiple-choice polls can be used to start icebreaker activities. For example, asking the question, Who was born during January? (followed by February to December) can help the class start to find common ground. The subsequent questions could go deeper into the learners' backgrounds. You could also keep the new class moving around the room with a selection of true or false questions. The golden rule of using any edtech platform is that you should always test your poll before unleashing it on your pollsters.

Orientation questions can also be carried out simply and memorably through polls. For example, the teacher could ask an open-ended question, 'Say one thing about volcanoes', then display the results in a word cloud or text wall. This would then offer many opportunities for enquiry learning about the causes of volcanic eruptions.

Image 43.1 Infographic: benefits of using Poll Everywhere

Diagnostic tests

There are, of course, many ways to poll learners to gauge their prior knowledge, level of understanding or revision needs. SurveyMonkey and Kahoot! offer visually appealing ways of polling and produce analytics that can clarify interventions and direct strategies.

Parents' evenings and events

Teachers could display the code to join a poll throughout a parents' evening or event. They could also email and text the code to parents and ask them to complete the poll immediately after the session.

Poll within PowerPoint

Google Slides allows teachers to create and conduct polls within a presentation. Chapter 49 on PowerPoint looks at some ways that teachers can create inclusive, learner-centred experiences by using presentations to project thought-provoking stimulus material, activities or flipped learning activities.

If you discover that you and your learners have taken to this tool, you could discover some more tips and resources in the Poll Everywhere community.

For learners

Learners may be drawn towards the anonymity of Poll Everywhere. They may also like the feeling of power that is accorded to them when polled on their feelings, opinions and prior knowledge. The results can be projected on to the board, so it is likely to encourage learners to feel that their input has been worth it.

The level of interactivity can increase engagement and levels of enjoyment. There are multiple ways in which polls can be carried out in a potentially immersive way, some of which are summarised below.

How to use Poll Everywhere

Before going into detail, here is a simple guide to get started.

- Create questions.

- Invite the audience.

- Display the results.

How to respond

Participants may respond via the website, by entering the URL that is visible on your poll. They can respond by sending a text message to the number displayed.

Poll Everywhere for assessment

The following can be ways to check understanding or provide oral assessment:

- directed questioning: based on poll results;

- rank order: to develop high-order thinking, place responses in order of importance and give reasons;

- surveys: diagnose gaps in learning;

- open-ended questions: build independence and encourage metacognition by asking students why they answered in that way.

Clickable image polls

These work best either on two separate screens or viewable on the one screen, split into two. Though the example in Image 43.2 is somewhat frivolous, the questions on the clickable image can be progressively more challenging.

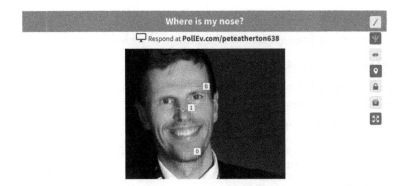

Image 43.2 For a bonus point, where is my chin?

Poll Everywhere for learning

Like Slido and Kahoot!, Poll Everywhere is an audience response system. Unlike Kahoot!, Poll Everywhere is often used in presentations and lectures. In that respect it could be seen to suit a 'command style' of the spectrum of teaching styles (Capel et al., 2016). There are, however, a range of more learner-centred and thought-provoking ways of using Poll Everywhere.

Word clouds

Like Google search results, word clouds open up potentially thought-provoking lines of enquiry. To help learners' discrimination skills, there will be a great deal of extraneous or redundant detail and hence they should be treated with caution (McComiskey 2015). Moreover, frequency of use does not always equate with significance (Atherton, 2017). Word clouds can, however, create abstractions that can develop critical thinking skills and help learners pursue enlightening lines of enquiry (Barrass, 2005). The key is to ask the learners to be critical of both the method and the results and interrogate what they reveal, what they do not reveal and why.

Multiple-choice polls

As with other response systems, Poll Everywhere polls gather both quantitative and qualitative data. If misused, these can provide results that are redundant, even misleading. Polls can, however, rise above straightforward low-order questions. The teacher will need to spend time planning questions that move towards achieving the mastery goals of the lesson (Hattie, 2009).

Links to the Teachers' Standards

S1: Set high expectations which inspire, motivate and challenge pupils

Learners can be converted from passive recipients of presentations to active participants. Poll Everywhere can be embedded into PowerPoint for Mac, Keynote (a real-time audience engagement app) and Google Slides.

S2: Promote good progress and outcomes by pupils

The teacher can build from low-order diagnostic questions to open-ended, high-order questions.

S5: Adapt to the strengths and needs of all pupils

Poll Everywhere can help teachers plan differentiated questions and test the effectiveness of differentiated learning objectives.

S6: Make accurate and productive use of assessment

Poll Everywhere can be used to identify misconceptions: if a high percentage of learners answer a question incorrectly, it can inform future planning.

S8: Fulfil wider professional responsibilities

Polling can provide evidence of parental engagement and can generate empirical evidence for managers and stakeholders. The trend for 'you said, we did' boards in the 2010s emphasises the importance of acting on student feedback.

References

Atherton, P (2017) *Kahoot for Assessment*. Liverpool: Kindle. Available at: https://www.amazon.co.uk/Using-Kahoot-Assessment-teachers-learners-ebook/dp/B071CJSTC4/ref=sr_1_1?ie=UTF8&qid=1492696884&sr=8-1&keywords=pete+atherton [accessed 11 July 2017].

Barrass, R (2005) *Students Must Write: A Guide to Better Writing in Coursework and Examinations (Routledge Study Guides)*, 3rd edition. London: Routledge.

Capel, S, Leask, M, Younie, S (2016) *Learning to Teach in the Secondary School*, 7th edition. London: Routledge.

Hattie, J (2009) *Visible Learning: A Synthesis of Over 800 Meta-Analyses Relating to Achievement*. New York: Routledge.

McComiskey, B (2015) *Dialectical Rhetoric by Bruce Mccomiskey (2015-07-01)*. Salt Lake City, UT: Utah State University Press.

44
Plickers

What are Plickers?

'Plickers' is yet another *portmanteau* word (like Instagram and Pinterest), which blends 'paper' and 'clickers'. These paper clickers work like any student response system insofar as the teacher asks a question and receives an instant response. If your school has a blanket ban on mobile devices in the classroom, Plickers could be a way for you to create live formative assessment data by using only your smartphone. In a similar way to QR codes, each Plickers card displays a code that can be read by the teacher's smartphone. Though it is generally used for quick checks on understanding, like all edtech tools it can be deployed to develop deep thinking and mastery.

What can Plickers do for teachers and learners?

For teachers

One of the sloganistic statements on the website is, 'focus more on teaching, less on setup'. There is, indeed, a low-tech simplicity to Plickers. The only device needed is the teacher's phone; there is no need for the school to invest in clickers that will surely become obsolete in a short space of time.

For learners

Teachers can often make the mistake of assuming that their learners will be comfortable with new technology. They will certainly be dismissive of handsets like clickers that will age quickly. With that in mind, Plickers offers a partial solution to situations where the technology can hinder, not enhance, the learning. Because learners are likely to grasp how to use Plickers very quickly, this should minimise the anxiety they can sometimes feel when they are unfamiliar with new technology. All they need to do is think, rotate the Plicker and hold it up so it can be read by the camera.

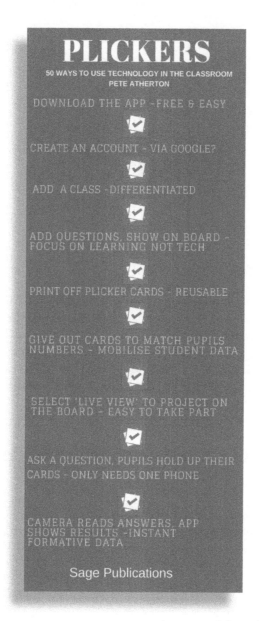

Image 44.1 Infographic: benefits of using Plickers

How to use Plickers

Here is a step-by-step guide to Plickers:

1. Download the Plickers app to your smartphone.

   The app is available from iTunes for iPad and iPhone or Google Play for Android devices. Make sure that you are signed in to the app.

2. On your tablet or classroom PC, create an account through Plickers.com, or sign in if you already have an account.

3. Add a new class and the names of the learners in each class. All learners will be assigned a number, which will match their Plicker card.

4. Click or tap 'Library' to locate your questions. Add new questions.

5. Once your questions have been added, you can project them on the whiteboard.

6. Locate Plickers cards here: **https://www.plickers.com/cards**.

   There is a choice of Plickers cards, e.g. the 'standard' set of 40 cards, which arranges two cards per sheet of A4. The cards can be used for multiple classes.

7. Print the cards: print on white card. The app on your phone will not be able to read the cards if they are too worn or have been laminated.

8. Give each learner the card that matches the number from the app.

9. Select 'live view' on the classroom PC, so the class can see the questions.

10. Ask a question and instruct the class to hold up their card. Learners will rotate their card to display the letter that corresponds to what they think is the correct answer.

11. Use your camera to read each card.

12. The answers will be displayed next to each learner's name. Also, a bar chart will indicate the percentage who selected each answer and how many were correct.

Plickers for assessment

As Plickers links each learner to a number, this presents opportunities for teachers to differentiate. For example, you can think about the number that you would give each learner. You can then sort by card number. That way, you could link the numbers to specific aspects of differentiation.

Perhaps the real skills involved in using Plickers with your learners lies in the planning of supplementary questions and follow-up activities to develop extra scaffolding and metacognition. These should ensure that your lessons do not become caught in a low-order thinking trap of multiple-choice answers.

Plickers for learning

Digital humans

The way that Plickers treads a fine line between digital and analogue technologies crystallises some debates about the efficacy of digital learning. Edtech can be viewed as a consuming force, that absorbs users into a horizontal, amorphous mass (Portanova, 2015). Plickers could be a welcome antidote to the ubiquity of digital technologies in education. From the learners' point of view, all they need to do is to look at the board, turn their cards and write down answers. They also need to think.

To examine this more vividly, it may be worth considering the 'resistance' stance to technology – where new technologies interfere with learning and de-skill (Leander, 2009). One of the causes of this de-skilling could be the visually cluttered nature of people's experience of new technologies (Page, 2014). Again, Plickers could occupy a more neutral space in which learners have temporary respite from digital devices.

To an extent, can teachers limit themselves professionally when they are either too evangelical or hostile towards edtech?

Links to the Teachers' Standards

S1: Set high expectations which inspire, motivate and challenge pupils

The design of supplementary questions and follow-up activities will help stretch and challenge and will reduce the risk of too many low-order questions.

S2: Promote good progress and outcomes by pupils

Plickers is a quick and accurate way of understanding prior knowledge.

S4 Plan and teach well-structured lessons

Plickers at the start and the end of lessons can provide clear evidence of learning having taken place. It can also clarify the teacher's next steps.

S5: Adapt to the strengths and needs of all pupils

The fact that you can number each student helps you organise the class in relation to student data.

S6: Make accurate and productive use of assessment

What will you do with the data once you have seen it? What support and interventions could the results help you put in place, both inside and outside the lessons?

S7: Manage behaviour effectively to ensure a good and safe environment

Teachers would have to make expectations clear to encourage good care of the Plicker cards, minimise disruption and ensure that there was no cheating.

S8: Fulfil wider professional responsibilities

Your learners could share their enjoyment of Plickers with their parents. Also, the immediacy and free nature of the formative data would pacify senior leaders.

References

Leander, D (2009) cited in Carrington, V, Robinson, M (eds.) *Digital Literacies: Social Learning and Classroom Practices*. London: SAGE.

Page, R (2014) *Researching Language and Social Media: A Student Guide*. Student Edition. London: Routledge.

Portanova, S (2015) The genius and the algorithm: reflections on the new aesthetic as a computer's vision. *Postdigital Aesthetics*, pp96–108. Available online at: https://link.springer.com/chapter/10.1057/9781137437204_8 [accessed 27 July 2017].

45
ClassDojo

What is ClassDojo?

ClassDojo is a sophisticated and carefully branded learning platform. Though it is not a formative assessment tool, it is designed to facilitate real-time formative assessment and improve classroom management. It is better suited to a primary/elementary school environment, with its bright colour scheme and friendly icons. It could also be appropriate for secondary/high school at Year 7; ClassDojo's reward system for behaviour could also suit team-based projects for older learners. Similar platforms are emerging all the time, for example, RedCritter, who position themselves as 'the ClassDojo alternative'.

What can ClassDojo do for teachers and learners?

For teachers

Before evaluating the uses of ClassDojo for teachers, it is worth mentioning that whole schools can choose to adopt ClassDojo. To do this, you would need to consult with the senior leadership team, the IT department and parents' groups. School leaders may feel that ClassDojo makes it easy to have a joined-up strategy for school values, learner voice and parental engagement.

Building a classroom community

ClassDojo encourages parental engagement by allowing learners to share their own photos of their school experiences with parents. These photos are essentially an eportfolio, or a digital equivalent of primary (or elementary) children gleefully brandishing their work at the school gates. At secondary level too, these eportfolios can give parents instant evidence of their child's progress and engagement.

Creating a positive learning culture

Teachers can instant message their learners and praise them for achieving well, for kindness, hard work or anything else that they feel is appropriate.

Image 45.1 Infographic: benefits of using ClassDojo

For learners

Learners can register as a student but they can also join a class with a code in a similar way to Kahoot! or Goformative. They can be sent digital high fives by their teachers for effort, achievement or positive behaviour.

Image 45.2 Found in translation? Digital high fives

Learners can view how many high fives they or their colleagues have received. This is revealed as a gamified interface, with an icon to represent each learner and a number to indicate their number of high fives.

ClassDojo prefers to emphasise rewarding positive behaviour but learners can also have points deducted for poor behaviour. These sanctions can sometimes be for slightly nebulous transgressions like 'disrespect' but they could also be for more clear-cut misdemeanours, for example, 'playing on your phone' or 'being late to class'.

How to use ClassDojo

If you sign up as a teacher, you enter the name of your school, grade/level/year and you also give your class a name. You can import a whole class from a list on your computer. For example clicking 'settings' in the top right corner displays a drop-down menu that enables teachers to connect students to each other and students with their parents.

Creating and sharing a digital portfolio

A digital portfolio (or eportfolio) can be created in three steps: firstly, learners will log into their class, then download the ClassDojo app. When students have done this, they can open the app, select 'student', then scan the QR code to log into the app (see Chapter 32 on QR codes).

Image 45.3 Caught green-handed – joining via QR code

ClassDojo for assessment

If ClassDojo exists to manage and monitor learner behaviour, could it also be used to assess work? One of the statistics listed on ClassDojo's website is that 95% of feedback given on ClassDojo is positive (**ideas.ClassDojo.com**). With that in mind, here are some suggestions for how ClassDojo could help with formative assessment.

Custom rewards

Teachers can set up some custom rewards and relate them to specific tasks. Learners could peer-assess in pairs, the teacher could read the work, then reward learners for qualities like openness, creativity, accuracy, metacognition and persistence (Beach, 2015).

Another way to use custom rewards is by linking learners' performance to exam board grading criteria for GCSE and BTEC. For example, if the teacher opens up the class, selects 'skills' then 'new skill', the teacher could create skills that match exam specifications. That way, ClassDojo could be a useful formative assessment tool and could help clarify and reinforce otherwise dry and complex grading criteria.

ClassDojo for learning: 'big ideas'

ClassDojo's ambitious branding extends as far as encouraging teachers and learners to embrace 'big ideas', like 'growth mindset' and mindfulness. The 'big ideas' pages on the ClassDojo website contain videos and related games and activities.

Growth mindset

There are a multitude of ways in which Dweck's (2012) notion of growth mindset could be explored through ClassDojo. One of ClassDojo's videos is entitled 'The Incredible Power of Yet'. This is a reference to Dweck's (2012) notion that it benefits children's wellbeing and achievement if they are told not that they cannot do something but they are unable to do it 'yet'. This progression from the 'fixed' to the 'growth' mindset can have a powerful effect on challenging people's negative and judgemental internal monologues, according to Dweck (2012). This thinking has been developed in the context of mathematics by Boaler and Dweck (2016), who emphasised the importance of embracing mistakes and struggle as essential parts of the learning process and in improving wellbeing and cognition.

Links to the Teachers' Standards

S1: Set high expectations which inspire, motivate and challenge pupils

S1c: Demonstrate consistently the positive attitudes, values and behaviour which are expected of pupils

This is essentially the *raison d'être* of ClassDojo.

S6: Make accurate and productive use of assessment

If the skills are adapted to match grading criteria, ClassDojo can be a fun way of visualising formative assessment.

S7: Manage behaviour effectively to ensure a good and safe environment

ClassDojo can help teachers establish clear routines, promote courteous behaviour and use sanctions and rewards appropriately.

S8: Fulfil wider professional responsibilities

ClassDojo embraces and promotes mindfulness and growth mindset through videos, games and online activities. The tagline on their website in June 2017 was 'Happier Classrooms'; all their resources and activities are intended to create a learning community characterised by positivity.

References

Beach, R (2015) *Using Apps for Learning Across the Curriculum*. London: Routledge.

Boaler, J, Dweck, C (2016) *Mathematical Mindsets: Unleashing Students' Potential through Creative Math*. Hoboken, NJ: John Wiley.

Dweck, C (2012) *Mindset*. London: Robinson.

Presentation platforms

46
Explain Everything

What is Explain Everything?

Launched in Poland in 2011, Explain Everything is an online interactive whiteboard and presentation tool that helps people pass on their knowledge and skills. By December 2016, they boasted 840,000 monthly users (Biggs, 2016). It is essentially an app, which markets itself as akin to a Swiss army knife in terms of its compactness and versatility. This is reflected in its broad demographic, which ranges from kindergarten to universities and the corporate market.

What can Explain Everything do for teachers and learners?

For teachers

Teachers can be as creative as a busy schedule will allow. Explain Everything's diverse functionality encompasses animation, audio and video editing, presentations and games. The materials teachers create can be from a blank canvas or derived from their own learning resources.

Presentation templates: explainer videos

Explainer videos are short, accessible instructional pieces of visual content; they can be comprised of pre-prepared video materials or they can mirror a teacher's live demonstration through a tablet. In some ways, adding an audio commentary to some slides is very similar to PowerPoint's dominant offering. Airplay through Apple TV enables teachers to display the contents of their tablet on the school's whiteboard. That means that any presentation software can be accessed on an iPad and can endow teachers with the gift of movement around the classroom. Explainer videos are dealt with in more detail in the section on assessment.

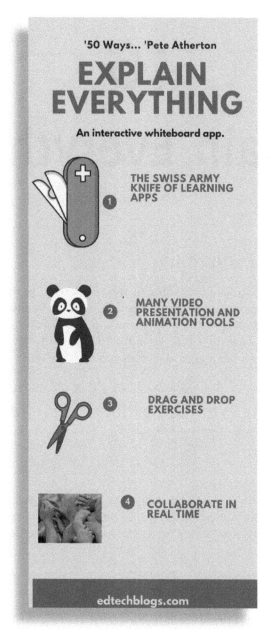

Image 46.1 Infographic: benefits of using Explain Everything

Interactive game templates

Teachers can easily create labelling or match exercises for their learners. The teacher can build the activities from a template, for example by matching Clipart images with bars containing text. The learners would participate by moving the objects on their tablet.

For learners

Real-time collaboration: create group accounts

Once you have signed in, go to 'account settings'. As you will be administrator, you will have the permissions to add a group account. Receivers will receive an email to activate their account.

Brainstorming

Here the emphasis is on learning not being a linear process. Though brainstorming can be used in a linear way – by recording lectures or importing worksheets – it can be more fruitful if used more organically.

How to use Explain Everything

Explain Everything offers a free 30-day trial. After that, there are three pricing options: individual (£24.99 per year at the time of writing), business (£49.99 a year) and enterprise (for 50+ 'team members', the price for which is available on request).

Create group accounts

Once you have signed in, go to 'account settings'. As you will be administrator, you will have the permissions to/ add a group account. Receivers will receive an email to activate their account. Another way of doing this is by sending a code to all users, which they enter in a box, similar to Goformative and Spiral.

The Explain Everything Discover pages contain more information than can be accommodated into this chapter.

Design

With design, you can create animations by using the draw tool, then dictate basic movements through the hand tool.

The hand tool also permits annotation of videos, similar to H5P or EDpuzzle. The example below shows the results of drawing and writing with the hand tool to explain specific aspects of a piece of video content.

Record

The appeal of this feature is that it can effectively capture learners' thoughts as they happen. Learners can draw ideas or answers, turn them into basic animations and edit them along a timeline.

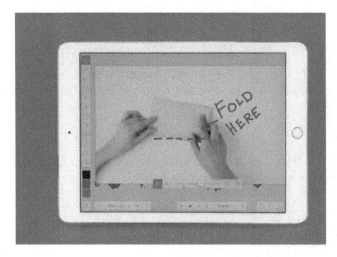

Image 46.2 Edtech gets hands on with Explain Everything

Explain Everything for assessment

Real-time collaboration

Teachers can upload their activities and choose to 'broadcast' a session with their class. To do this, they select the 'collaboration' tab on the 'home' screen and the learners then join by entering a code. The class can be set individual tasks or asked to revise together or solve problems collaboratively.

Quick capture

Learners will have the capacity to capture, then share their work.

Explainer videos

Quick, short, accessible screencasts can be powerful ways of showing learning having taken place. The teacher can then enter into dialogue with the learner about the work by making annotations via the tablet's keyboard.

Explain Everything for learning

The fact that Explain Everything has such a broad range of features suggests that it belongs to that breed of edtech that aims to create immersive, meandering educational experiences. In that respect, the tool can be part of a *rhizomatic* learning culture (Cormier, 2011). While a connectivist classroom embraces the notion of knowledge as negotiated along a fluid continuum (Siemens, 2005), rhizomatic learning adopts a botanical metaphor. In botany, the rhizome has no centre and its multiple shoots grow in many directions. When a learning experience is rhizomatic, it has no fixed destination and embraces diversions and digressions.

It could be argued, therefore, that Explain Everything's diverse functionality and learner-centred immersiveness belong in an age in which knowledge is constantly moving. In that respect, it is not alone in this book, as several edtech platforms embrace learning on tablets in ways that position the learner as the co-creator of knowledge that is likely to have become obsolete within a short space of time.

Links to the Teachers' Standards

S1: Set high expectations which inspire, motivate and challenge pupils

Collaborative learning and editing in real time require diplomatic, maybe learner-centred contracting.

S2: Promote good progress and outcomes by pupils

Learners' own explainer videos and collaborative exercises can be a memorable way to build on prior knowledge.

S5: Adapt to the strengths and needs of all pupils

Feedback can be assigned to individuals or pairs based on their data and recent performance. The rhizomatic nature of the learning can create openings for learners to exceed their expectations. The sheer variety of opportunities for learners to express themselves through Explain Everything can enable teachers to show awareness of the factors that can inhibit learning.

S6: Make accurate and productive use of assessment

There are a multitude of formative assessment options, for example, students being asked to make explainer videos, presentations, animated explainer videos or stories.

S7: Manage behaviour effectively to ensure a good and safe environment

Group work can enable teachers to reward the learners for working harmoniously and producing impressive work.

S8: Fulfil wider professional responsibilities

Learning about edtech platforms like Explain Everything can create a more proactive attitude to continuing professional development.

References

Biggs, J (2016) *Explain Everything, the Digital Whiteboard, Raises $3.7 Million to Bring Learning to the iPad.* TechCrunch. Available online at: https://techcrunch.com/2016/12/15/explaineverything-the-digital-whiteboard-raises-3-7-million-to-bring-learning-to-the-ipad/ [accessed 26 June 2017].

Cormier, D (2011) *Rhizomatic Learning – Why we teach? – Dave's Educational Blog.* Davecormier.com. Available at: http://davecormier.com/edblog/2011/11/05/rhizomatic-learning-why-learn/ [accessed 26 June 2017].

Siemens, G (2005) *A Learning Theory for the Digital Age.* Available online at: http://devrijeruimte.org/content/artikelen/Connectivism.pdf [accessed 27 October 2016].

47
Infographics

What are infographics?

Simply information presented in the form of graphics, the use of infographics is increasingly commonplace on social media platforms such as Pinterest. In terms of their applications to teaching and learning, infographics can be a powerful addition to the visual learning arsenal. There are numerous free infographic tools on the internet, for example, Vizualize.me, Piktochart and Venngage.

This chapter will focus on making infographics with Canva. Canva is a design and graphics website. If you want to create flyers, brochures and bar graphs, edit photos or carry out any conceivable design task, Canva provides design templates, complete with graphics and a bank of photos. Many of the designs are free; others are premium products, retailing at around $1 each.

What can infographics do for teachers and learners?

For teachers

Learning objectives

Have you ever thought that displaying learning objectives in bullet-point form on a PowerPoint neither informs nor inspires the learners? Presented as an infographic, the objectives can be juxtaposed to explanatory images. The infographics can be as playful and witty as you feel is appropriate.

Activity sheets

Reading activity sheets can lead to learners complaining that they are confused. One of the reasons for this can be that activity sheets or worksheets are sometimes too verbose and overcomplicated. Infographics can help you get straight to the point.

Image 47.1 Infographic: benefits of using infographics

Revision resources

A considerable amount of information can be compressed into a single infographic. Infographics can also use the interplay of arresting words, numbers, images and graphics to facilitate an understanding of topics and issues.

For learners

Revision resources

Either working in pairs or alone, in or out of class, creating infographics can add a level of customisation to learners' revision. If the aesthetics and the information are selected by the learner, that can provide an engaging level of autonomy.

Poster presentations

Poster presentations are frequently used in universities by students and academics. At secondary or further education level, infographics are an alternative to the threat of text-heavy 'death by PowerPoint'. In the absence of voluminous text in bullet-point form, learners have to explain the content, which necessitates a certain level of preparation and understanding.

Classroom resources

The learner-generated infographics would be useful memory aids if they adorned the classroom walls or corridors, the virtual learning environment, departmental blog, social media page – even students' bedroom walls when they are revising.

How to make infographics on Canva

Below is a step-by-step guide to creating infographics on Canva.

1. Visit **Canva.com**.

2. Select '+More' (in the top right of the screen).

3. Click 'Infographic',

4. Select a 'Canva layout' from the left sidebar.

5. When you can see your chosen layout (on the right), edit the text by clicking on it and typing your own words.

6. Use the menu on the far left to help you choose a layout, some elements (for example, free photos, shapes and charts), custom text, a different background or even one of your own image files.

7. When you are satisfied with your creation, select 'download' at the very top of the screen. This will save your infographic as a PNG file in your downloads folder.

Infographics for assessment

Summaries

If you want to provide a 'story so far', infographics can provide a springboard for the learners to demonstrate that learning has taken place. They can also offer opportunities to address misconceptions or clarify any confusion or gaps in knowledge. Summary infographics can also lead the teachers to 'reach' or stretch and challenge questions.

Infographics for learning

Not only do infographics enable learners to see and communicate an overview of a topic, they can elucidate complex data and encourage new ways of thinking about information (Guzzetti, 2016). Subsequently, creating infographics can foster high-order thinking and make deeper learning more achievable, as they improve decision making and strengthen memory (Heer et al., 2010).

Infographics and literacy

If learners are to create effective infographics, they will need to employ careful selection skills, and defend their sources as being credible and relevant. The skills of interpreting and discriminating are also essential both to the creation of infographics and the development of literacy (Davidson, 2014, cited in Guzzetti, 2016).

Links to the Teachers' Standards

S1: Set high expectations which inspire, motivate and challenge pupils

One way of doing this is by setting Bloom's taxonomy as a template (Bloom et al., 1956). That way, learners will be encouraged to select information that is designed to show that they have remembered then understood, applied, analysed and evaluated. The images, graphics and numbers would help them demonstrate the more high-order task of creating.

S2: Promote good progress and outcomes by pupils

Infographics can be used for self- or peer assessment.

S3: Demonstrate good subject and curriculum knowledge

Infographics can help demonstrate the clarity and depth of your subject knowledge.

S4: Plan and teach well-structured lessons

Infographics can make for memorable learning experiences.

S6: Make accurate and productive use of assessment

Infographics can reveal the breadth and depth of learners' understanding, both in the form or the text, images, numbers and graphics that they create and the presentations that they deliver. As infographics are easy to edit, learners should be clear about how to highlight the successes and act of feedback in the form of verbal guidance, sticky notes, annotations or social media comments.

References

Bloom, BS, Engelhart, MD, Furst, EJ, Hill, WH, Krathwohl, DR (1956) *Taxonomy of Educational Objectives: The Classification of Educational Goals*. Handbook I: Cognitive domain. New York: David McKay.

Guzzetti, B (2016) *Handbook of Research on the Societal Impact of Digital Media*. Hershey, PA: Information Science Reference.

Heer, J, Bostock, M, Ogievetsky, V (2010) *Through the Visualization Zoo*. Queueacm. Available online at: http://delivery.acm.org/10.1145/1750000/1743567/p59-heer.pdf?ip=82.41.43.234&id=1743567& acc=OPEN&key=4D4702B0C3E38B35.4D4702B0C3E38B35.4D4702B0C3E38B35.6D218144511F343 7&CFID=752307665&CFTOKEN=41052242&__acm__=1492513126_4433dd64b4e6c92b5f27366465 20d783 [accessed 18 April 2017].

48
Canva

What is Canva?

If you were wondering how all the infographics in this book were made, the answer – on Canva! A cursory look at Canva will reveal that it is so much more than a tool for making infographics (see separate chapter (47) specifically on infographics). It is a wide-ranging set of online graphic design templates that facilitate quick, easy and attractive documents. There are too many to discuss in depth here but some notable examples are magazine covers, photo collages, presentations, ebooks and blog graphics.

What can Canva do for teachers and learners?

For teachers

You may find it very appealing to use Canva to summarise or present information, both during lessons and as part of additional resources. Depending on your view of the extent to which teachers should model examples of completed work, you could use ready-made templates to provide an idea of what the learners' work might look like. The point, of course, would be to use the activity to develop, deepen, apply or revise knowledge.

The following could be attractive and engaging ways to use Canva in the classroom:

- infographics;
- blog graphics;
- letterheads;
- magazines;
- resumés.

In addition to these, it is worth looking at Canva for Education. Here you can find some more highly user-friendly teaching graphs, for instance:

- Venn diagrams;

- bar graphs;

- organisation charts.

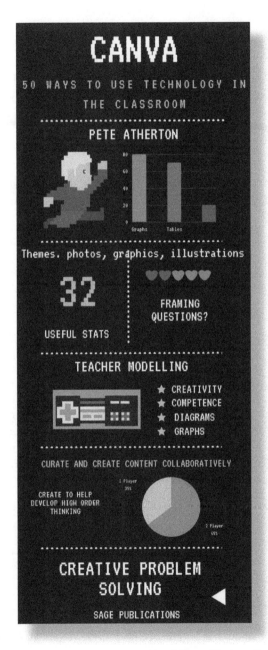

Image 48.1 Infographic: benefits of Canva (how very meta!)

Easy-to-follow guidance on how to use Canva's myriad features can be found on their teaching materials page: **https://designschool.canva.com/teaching-materials/**. In addition, there are some lesson plans, some of which will be referred to in the 'Canva for assessment' section: **http://askatechteacher.com/2017/02/28/13-ways-to-use-canva-in-your-classroom/**.

For learners

Curate content

As with Pinterest and Tumblr, Canva allows for a great deal of sourcing and recontextualising relevant (or irrelevant) content. There are thousands of images and graphics to choose from; many are free but sometimes learners may be driven to pay $1 for a stock image that fits their creation perfectly.

Work in a team

Signing up to Canva grants members free access to a team of up to ten people. This opens up many opportunities for collaborative enterprises, for example, the creation of ebooks or tri-fold brochures.

Tumblr posts

Please see Chapter 22 on Tumblr as an aid to teaching and learning. In many ways, Canva helps develop essential multimodal literacies that are essential for the digital age (Duckworth and Ade-Ojo, 2014).

How to use Canva

The example I will be working with is how to create a Tumblr graphic.

Once you have registered, click 'create a design', then choose from the range of templates. If you select 'Tumblr graphic', you will see a selection of Canva layouts in the left sidebar. Drag the one you want over to the space in the centre. You can then manipulate your template by dragging text, images, backgrounds and your own files across to your new design. When you are happy with how it all looks, click 'download' and it will save as a PNG picture file.

Despite this helpful advice on how to use Canva, there is superior guidance on the website, as a short 'how to' video.

Canva for assessment

Award badges and certificates

Learners gain a significant amount of confidence from being rewarded. Canva can be used to make visually impressive awards to recognise achievement and effort.

Infographics, brochures, blogs, social media posts and charts

Reframing information in different graphical forms cannot happen without some concerted flipped learning or concentrated teaching activities. Most activities like these require high-order thinking skills like applying, evaluating, creating (Churches, 2014); they also necessitate the use of creative problem solving, prioritising, discriminating, proofreading and editing.

Canva for learning

Teaching creativity

Canva encourages a great deal of creative freedom and experimentation. It can be easy for teachers to assume that their learners will be competent in and comfortable with creativity. In scientific subjects that are deemed less creative (mistakenly, of course), the skills of scientific questions and the circuitous, problematical route to answers can be practised (Starko, 2010). With that in mind, it may be worth embracing a culture of problem finding, instead of being excessively prescriptive about intended outcomes (Starko, 2010). When the creative task has been completed, teachers might want to see this as the beginning, not the end. This echoes Papert's (1991) notion of *constructionism*, in which artefacts created by learners are intended to stimulate thought that is relevant to their own context (Sullivan, 2017).

If learners' own context is enmeshed in social media communication, tools like Canva offer a chance for young people to progress from being 'app-dependent' to 'app-enabled'. Assessed activities and assignments that use Canva could potentially empower learners to create their own critical and sophisticated digital identities (Vosen Callens, 2014). The lingering issue, though, is how far activities such as these can de-skill and effectively neuter the traditional literacies that are still required to read, understand and pass exams.

Links to the Teachers' Standards

S1: Set high expectations which inspire, motivate and challenge pupils

Canva's templates can encourage supportive, collaborative working. The autonomy given to learners means that you will be unlikely to run out of rewarding, meaningful extension tasks for high attainers. Teachers can make neat rewards for learners to recognise their achievement or effort.

S4: Plan and teach well-structured lessons

Canva's variety is your variety.

S5: Adapt to the strengths and needs of all pupils

The creation of teams is a good opportunity to differentiate.

(Continued)

(Continued)

S6: Make accurate and productive use of assessment

The convenient thing about Canva is how easy it is to prove that feedback has been given and acted upon. Teachers can make templates to facilitate this process, for example.

S8: Fulfil wider professional responsibilities

All documents are easily exported as a PNG or PDF or shared on social media, so there are many ways to celebrate learners' work.

References

Churches, A (2014) *Bloom's analyzing.* Available online at: ttps://edorigami.wikispaces.com/ [accessed 23 April 2014].

Duckworth, V, Ade-Ojo, G (2014) *Landscapes of Specific Literacies in Contemporary Society.* London: Routledge.

Papert, S (1991) Preface. In Harel, I, Papert, S (eds.) *Constructionism, Research Reports and Essays, 1985–1990.* Norwood, NJ: Ablex, p1.

Starko, A (2010) *Creativity in the Classroom.* New York: Routledge.

Sullivan, F (2017) *Creativity, Technology, and Learning.* New York: Routledge.

Vosen Callens, M (2014) Using Bloom's taxonomy to teach course content and improve social media literacy. *Journal of Interdisciplinary Studies in Education,* 3(1): 1–25.

49
PowerPoint

What is PowerPoint?

Yes, PowerPoint! It may be the end of the 2010s but PowerPoint is still the default tool for presentations. Indeed, if someone says to you, 'Have you got your PowerPoint?', that person is using a *proprietary eponym*, in which the name of a brand is so dominant that it is used instead of the generic noun.

Before we go any further, it must be said that this chapter simply has to fight the good fight about how not to use PowerPoint. For that reason, part of the 'How to use PowerPoint' section will address 'How *not* to use PowerPoint'.

What can PowerPoint do for teachers and learners?

For teachers

Structuring lessons

Many teachers use presentation tools as a crutch in case they forget what is due to happen next in their lesson. PowerPoints can help ensure that you – and your learners – are clear about the lesson's objectives and success criteria.

Flipped learning presentations

Any PowerPoint that you produce can be saved under a different name, then edited so that the next lessons will be spent applying, reviewing, testing, hypothesising, maybe even creating.

For learners

There are numerous PowerPoint templates based on well-known TV game shows, for example, *Deal or No Deal* and *Who Wants to Be a Millionaire?* Games such as these promote team building and the sense of competition can be a motivating factor.

Image 49.1 Infographic: benefits of using PowerPoint

How to use PowerPoint (without boring your class)

How *not* to use PowerPoint

If you have an idle 30 minutes, take a look at SlideShare and make a list of what you do not like to see. You will almost certainly be assaulted by slides with too much small text, confusing diagrams with arrows pointing in several directions, text that is impossible to read against the ill-chosen image; a hallucinogenic colour scheme; slides that are cluttered by pointless Clipart, equally point-less transitions or animations. Many or all of us have been guilty of this, of course, and we will still experience these mistakes.

As an animation tool

To create basic animations (as opposed to pointless animated figures), simply choose your own or a copyright-free background image. Then add a transparent image to it. Duplicate the slide but each time make the second image larger and move it slightly. Repeat the process, then set the animation speed to 0.5 seconds.

PowerPoint for assessment

PowerPoint without a PowerPoint

This is a great way to ensure that learners can discriminate, understand, edit and deliver and it is all completed on paper. You can ask them to present five posters, cards or pieces of paper to summarise their initial understanding or revision. Each page must be limited to a small number of bullet points and a maximum of 40 words per 'slide'. If the learners are nervous, the 'presentations' could be performed as a 'marketplace' activity, through which small groups circulate around the class and summarise their findings on paper or an iPad application, for example, Classkick or Goformative.

Feedback can be provided after taking photographs and uploading to a cloud (Apple Education, G Suite, Padlet and so on). Alternatively, peer or teacher feedback could be given on a sticky note.

Learners' own presentations

When multiple learners or groups are instructed to present, it maintains the pace if each PowerPoint is stored in a cloud, for example, Google Slides or Padlet. This still does not address what the other learners are going to achieve whilst watching.

For this reason, it is desirable to direct students to ask questions using Google Slides or pool their questions into a Padlet wall. They could also have a structured worksheet to fill in while each presentation is happening. This worksheet would be a continuation of the initial guidelines and success criteria for the presentation.

This brings us to the style of teaching that you wish your learners to adopt. All too often, teachers find it acceptable for their learners to employ the 'command style' of teaching (Capel et al., 2009), based purely on instruction and where the audience are passive recipients. Among other styles, you may wish to consider the 'divergent discovery style', in which the learner-as-presenter would present alternative solutions to a problem and set tasks that ask the class to do the same. There would, of course, need to be clear guidelines and scaffolding for this method to work and it would work better if the learners were presenting in pairs. A short individual proposal at the start or evaluation at the end could clarify who did what, to help the teacher award grades.

The 'practice style' (Capel et al., 2009) could ask the learners-as-presenter to augment their presentation to generate relevant tasks, displayed clearly (in roughly size 30 font). The teacher would act as teaching assistant in this process. Again, the success criteria would have to be established first, to ensure that the task was achievable, pertinent and challenging.

PowerPoint for learning

Again, it may be judicious to discuss some negatives from the outset. Can the practice of delivering presentations de-skill and render learners passive and indisposed to deep thinking? Sorensen (2017) bemoans reducing university course content to *bullet point knowledge*. The introductory bullet points and, indeed, entire presentations are not peer-reviewed, so there is an issue with quality control.

Sorensen draws on Tufte's (2003) article, in which he challenges the tyranny of business culture in education, in which the skills of constructing explanatory sentences are replaced by linear, trivial and distracting visual stimuli.

Hill et al. (2012) develop these ideas with a sense of ambivalence: PowerPoint may reduce learner engagement and dumb down knowledge in a way that is at odds with the complexity of the outside world but there are some benefits. These are largely limited to learners' enjoyment of and expectations of seeing PowerPoint (Hill et al., 2012).

The sources above are concerned primarily with the higher education sector and are largely negative in tone. Could PowerPoint have a positive effect in secondary schools? If effective pedagogy involves clear structure and pace, appropriate questioning, differentiation, concept mapping and teacher modelling (Muijs and Reynolds, 2001), PowerPoint could aid successful teaching and learning. Slides can help create the structure and maintain the pace; a single slide can convey the required gravitas of a high-order question (duplicating the same slide can provide the necessary scaffolding).

Links to the Teachers' Standards

S1: Set high expectations which inspire, motivate and challenge pupils

If learners are to deal with their own nerves when giving presentations and learn something from their peers, they must agree on some common expectations.

If learners' own presentations are centred around questions based on stimulus material, this could be a powerful way to develop high-order thinking. Again, this would require learners working in well-chosen pairs or even trios.

S2: Promote good progress and outcomes by pupils

If learners have a responsibility to present to their peers and there are strict rules regarding format, structure and content, this could capitalise on previous knowledge.

S5: Adapt to the strengths and needs of all pupils

Interactive presentations like Google Slides enable learners to ask questions in real time for a plenary later or to be answered by their peers. Thinking carefully about groupings and the questions that teachers pose on their PowerPoints can ensure that the class is suitably differentiated.

S6: Make accurate and productive use of assessment

The section on 'PowerPoint for assessment' discusses various means of assessing work through presentations.

S8: Fulfil wider professional responsibilities

The support teachers give to learners who may be very nervous about presenting is crucial here.

References

Capel, S, Leask, M, Turner, T (2009) *Learning to Teach in the Secondary School*. London: Routledge.

Hill, A, Arford, T, Lubitow, A, Smollin, L (2012) I'm ambivalent about it. *Teaching Sociology*, 40(3): 242–256.

Muijs, D, Reynolds, D (2001) *Effective Teaching: Evidence and Practice*. London: SAGE.

Sorensen, B (2017) Let's ban PowerPoint in lectures – it makes students more stupid and professors more boring. *The Independent*. Available online at: http://www.independent.co.uk/news/education/lets-ban-PowerPoint-in-lectures-it-makes-students-more-stupid-and-professors-more-boring-a7597506.html [accessed 5 July 2017].

Tufte, E (2003) PowerPoint is evil. *Wired* 11.09. Available online at: http://web.archive.org/web/20140415121014/http://archive.wired.com/wired/archive/11.09/ppt2.html [accessed 5 July 2017].

50
iSpring

What is iSpring?

Before going into detail, it is important to note that iSpring is a paid suite of elearning tools designed for PowerPoint. There is, of course, a free trial available for a limited time and a range of free features.

This chapter will pay closer attention to the free products but will also browse the paid options to provide a little context.

What can iSpring do for teachers and learners?

For teachers

Free Quizmaker

The free version provides basic functionality. There are some interactive features that your learners may find engaging, for example, iSpring Quizmaker.

iSpring Free Cam

As an alternative to the likes of Panopto or Quicktime, you may be drawn towards the ability to record and edit screencasts and upload to YouTube.

Paid options: iSpring Flip

iSpring Flip converts a Word, PDF or PowerPoint file into an interactive ebook. Teachers are able to monitor the progress of each learner reading the ebook, though there will be ways for learners to click and scroll, instead of reading.

For learners

Learners and stakeholders may be impressed by the slick sophistication of the resources. If teachers and senior leaders compared notes on the preferred house style and conventions of these resources, they could ensure that they project the right values and ethos.

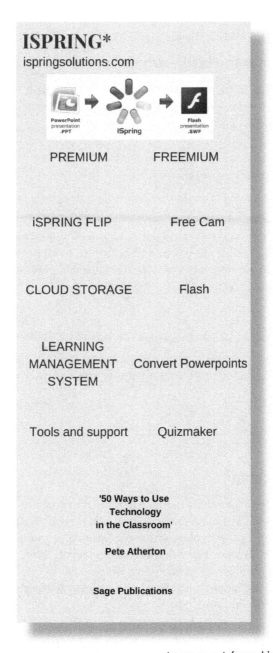

Image 50.1 Infographic: benefits of using iSpring

There is no doubt that iSpring is a sophisticated collection of tools and services. If your institution is considering purchasing iSpring, you may want to conduct a SWOT (strengths, weaknesses, opportunities and threats) analysis and a cost–benefit analysis. The conversations about benefits may need to focus on the extent to which iSpring could make the learning faster, deeper, more enjoyable for all. If all of these are true, does that still justify the outlay? Can any one edtech platform be transformative without a radical rethinking of training, allocation of funds and use of time (Jenkins et al., 2017)?

How to use iSpring

Convert PowerPoints to Flash – why?

You may want to do this if you are creating supporting resources or flipped lessons. If your PowerPoint is converted to a Flash file, it may be uploaded seamlessly and viewed on a virtual learning environment like Canvas or on YouTube.

iSpring for assessment

iSpring Free Cam

If you find this tool easy to use, you could put out content frequently to build engagement and create a sense of serendipity. Your videos could be posted on social media or sent via text from the school to pose a challenging question before class, scaffold a discovery learning task or provide mark schemes or assessment objectives.

PowerPoint to Flash

The key here is avoiding using these resources simply to transmit information. Make sure you review, test, ask questions, link to other assessment resources and make it clear to the learners what you want them to *do*.

iSpring for learning

Elearning or eteaching?

Blin and Munro (2008) feel that edtech can merely be used to replicate tried and tested pedagogies (cited in Kirkwood and Price, 2014). Moreover, Selwyn (2011) warns against a sometimes evangelical stance made by proponents of technology enhanced learning, without sufficient academic rigour. Hamilton and Friesen (2013) view this as *instrumentalism* (Bayne, 2014, p6). Instrumentalism views technology as a natural, ideologically neutral force which exists to help us reach pre-defined goals, for example, learning. Such thinking could be seen to suppress debate about how technology relates to education and culture (Bayne, 2014, p6).

If a teacher uses iSpring to convert a PowerPoint file to Flash, the teacher is more likely to have a file that is suitable for elearning. But what does this mean? Elearning goes deeper than that in terms of differentiation.

Lortie (1975, cited in Borg, 2004) talked about how trainee teachers have already acquired a reductionist perception of the teaching profession from their own time at school. This 'apprenticeship of observation' tends to make trainees follow safe, well-trodden paths. To what extent is their observation edtech part of the problem? To be successful in implementing these new and emerging technologies, teachers may need to break free from the apprenticeship of *digital* observation.

Links to the Teachers' Standards

S1: Stretch and challenge

The materials that you create will need to combine sufficient scaffolding with varied levels of challenge.

S2: Promote good progress and outcomes by pupils

Will learners be more likely to take pride in their work if the resources are slick and professional?

S4: Plan and teach well-structured lessons

The free quizzes and screencasts can add serendipity and increase engagement before, during and after lessons.

S5: Adapt to the strengths and needs of all pupils

You can build the levels of challenge into the quizzes, even provide clues if appropriate.

S6: Make accurate and productive use of assessment

There are basic forms of assessment through the activities on the PowerPoints but you can augment this with short videos made on iSpring Free Cam.

S8: Make a positive contribution to the wider life and ethos of the school

Stakeholders are likely to view impressive and publicly available resources as a step in the right direction.

References

Bayne, S (2014) What is the matter with technology enhanced learning? *Learning, Media and Technology,* DOI: 10.1080/17439884.2014.9158511. Available online at: http://www.tandfonline.com/doi/full/10.1080/17439884.2014.915851 [accessed 4 October 2017].

Borg, M (2004) A case study of the development in pedagogic thinking of a pre-service teacher. *TESL.* Available online at: http://www.tesl-ej.org/wordpress/issues/volume9/ej34/ej34a5/ [accessed 8 August 2017].

Hamilton, EC, Friesen, N (2013) Online education: a science and technology studies perspective. *Canadian Journal of Learning and Technology,* 39(2). http://cjlt.csj.ualberta.ca/index.php/cjlt/article/view/689.

Jenkins, M, Browne, T, Walker, R, Hewitt, R (2017) The development of technology enhanced learning: findings from a 2008 survey of UK higher education institutions. *Interactive Learning Environments,* 19(5). Available online at: http://www.tandfonline.com/doi/abs/10.1080/10494820903484429 [accessed 18 July 2017].

Kirkwood, A, Price, L (2014) Technology-enhanced learning and teaching in higher education: what is 'enhanced' and how do we know? A critical literature review. *Learning, Media and Technology,* 39(1): 6–36.

Selwyn, N (2011) Editorial: In praise of pessimism – the need for negativity in educational technology. *British Journal of Educational Technology,* 42(5), DOI: 10.1111/j.1467-8535.2011.01215.x

Index